HISTORY OF THE IRISH IN AMERICA

Ann Kathleen Bradley

HISTORY OF THE IRISH IN AMERICA

Ann Kathleen Bradley

CHARTWELL
BOOKS, INC.

A QUANTUM BOOK

Published by Chartwell Books
A Division of Book Sales Inc
114 Northfield Avenue
Edison, New Jersey 08837
USA

ISBN 0-7858-0731-4

This book was produced by
Quantum Books Ltd
6 Blundell Street
London N7 9BH

Printed in China by Leefung-Asco Printers Ltd

Contents

THE IRELAND
THEY LEFT

When Columbus reached the shores of the New World in 1492, one of his crewmen was William Eris, or Ayers, a native of Galway in Ireland. That sailor was only the first of the many thousands of Irish men and women who set out over the next several centuries to fulfill their dreams of a different life in America, a land that became for many of them the 'island of destiny' long sung by Irish bards.

Today, people of Irish descent in the United States outnumber those living in Ireland by three to one. But most of those who made the long voyage across the Atlantic nurtured a strong and enduring bond with their native land, and they kept its memory alive for themselves and for their children long after they had settled in their adopted country. The American Irish became, more than almost any other immigrant group, a people who dwelt in two worlds — loyal to their island homeland, but ready and eager to grasp the opportunities they found in America and carve out a better life for themselves in that dynamic new society.

The early Irish were a largely pastoral people, shepherds and herdsmen ruled by tribal chieftains. Beginning with King Henry II in 1171, however, English monarchs began to establish control over their island neighbor and introduce feudal practices including the manorial system. Gradually a system of small family farms developed. People lived in rural communities and raised grain, flax for linen, potatoes and livestock. Barter was the accepted mode of exchange, and when land was passed on it was divided among all the boys in a family.

When Oliver Cromwell's troops defeated the army of Charles Stewart following the rebellion of the 1640s, however, they forced thousands of Irish Catholics off their land, executed thousands more, and sent others to live in bleak, infertile western territories. Many more were transported as slaves to Virginia and the West Indies.

At the disastrous Battle of the Boyne in 1690, the deposed Catholic monarch James II and his French and Irish-Catholic soldiers were defeated by the new English King William III, commanding a German, English and Irish-Protestant army. The 1691 Treaty of Limerick allowed Irish-Catholic leaders and aristocracy to leave and promised that Catholics who remained in Ireland would suffer no persecution of discrimination. But British and Irish Protestants demanded vengeance, and during the 1690s the discriminatory Penal Laws were enacted by the British Parliament. Irish Catholics were not allowed to vote, hold office, sit in Parliament, serve in the government or the army forces, found schools, practice law, own weapons or purchase property. Their religious rights were also curtailed: Catholic bishops were exiled and religious orders outlawed, while Catholic priests could not enter the country or move about freely. The Penal Laws reduced the Irish Catholic majority — 75 percent of the population — to a subclass that held only five percent of the property and paid tithes to support the Protestant church and churchmen, while the Protestant minority owned 95 percent of the property and held all political power.

During the eighteenth and nineteenth centuries, England was extending her commercial dominance and needed wool for her mills. The Protestant landlords found it more profitable to combine the small farms their Catholic tenants rented from them into large estates to make room for sheep grazing. Many tenant farmers were forced off their lands. Rents grew ever more burdensome under the so-called 'rack-rent' system, and the Irish saw the products of their labor going increasingly to swell English profits in world markets, rather than to feed and clothe their families. Gradually, agrarian secret societies grew up to redress local economic grievances, and an underground guerrilla war raged between Irish peasants and their Protestant landlords. The failed revolution of 1798 was an attempt to end government repression in Ireland, but it only produced martyrs to the cause and the official incorporation of Ireland into the United Kingdom of Great Britain and Ireland. By the time the potato blight wiped out the basic subsistence food crop of Irish farmers in the 1840s, many saw no choice but to abandon a land that had caused them so much hardship, and resolutely set their sights on creating a better life in America. As they embarked, then, on a long and arduous ocean voyage that was only the beginning of the great Irish-American adventure, the land that they left seemed no longer to want them.

RIGHT *The 2,739-foot Purple Mountain near Killarney in County Kerry is the chief landmark in this beautiful lake district.*

LEFT *The Treaty of Limerick was signed on the Treaty Stone in 1691, which can still be seen.*

BELOW AND RIGHT *Irish emigrants to America left behind thatched cottages on tiny farms such as these in Donegal (below) and Galway (right).*

PAGES 12/13 *Peat, dug by hand from bogs, was the chief fuel in forest-poor Ireland.*

ABOVE *The Blarney Stone lies at the foot of the battlements of Blarney Castle in County Cork. Kissing the stone is alleged to confer the Irish gift of the gab.*

ABOVE *The Rock of Cashel in County Tipperary is the former seat of the Munster kings of Ireland. The huge, thirteenth-century cathedral that now crowns the rock is dedicated to "God, St. Patrick and St. Ailbhe".*

PAGES 16 AND 17 *Eight miles into the Atlantic Ocean off County Kerry, the Skellig Rocks support the remains of an isolated monastery established by St. Finian in the seventh century. It was abandoned in the twelfth century.*

LEFT *The largest group of prehistoric remains in Ireland is found near Carrowmore in County Sligo, in western Ireland.*

BELOW *The flat-topped mountain of Ben Bulben in County Sligo looms up behind Donegal Bay. The mountain is 1,730 feet high.*

RIGHT *One of Ireland's most celebrated holy sites is at Clonmacnois in eastern Ireland. It was here, on the banks of the River Shannon, that St. Ciaran founded a monastery in 548.*

ABOVE *Once host to Europe's large horse fair, Ballinasloe in County Galway today hosts the largest livestock fair in Ireland every October.*

ABOVE *Timoleague Abbey in County Cork is a Franciscan friary established in 1240. It was sacked by English troops in 1642, but the extensive ruins are still extant.*

ABOVE *Oppressive landlords were a fact of Irish life, symbolized by the great houses they built. Powerscourt in County Wicklow, built on 14,000 acres in the eighteenth century, is reached by a mile-long avenue.*

ABOVE *The town of Avoca is situated in the beautiful winding Vale of Avoca in County Wicklow.*

ABOVE *The Cliffs of Moher in County Clare rise 700 feet straight up*
from the sea. The county in southern Ireland is almost entirely
surrounded by water.

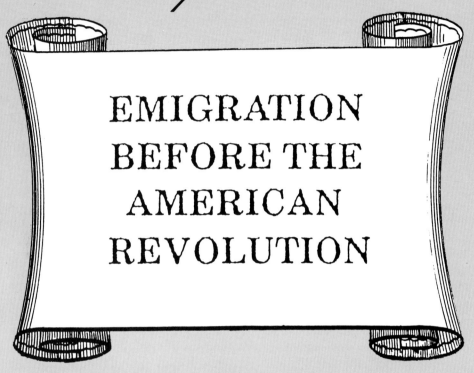

EMIGRATION BEFORE THE AMERICAN REVOLUTION

The Irish who followed Ayers to America were among the very first settlers and explorers. Francis Maguire was one of the residents of Jamestown, Virginia, in 1607, and John Coleman, an Irishman who sailed on Henry Hudson's *Half Moon,* was killed by Indians at Coleman's Point (now Sandy Hook) and buried on Coney Island. A wealthy Quaker merchant from Cork named Samuel Gookin brought a large group of settlers over from Ireland in 1621 and named the place where they landed New Port Newce (present-day Newport News) after his birthplace. And Darby Field discovered the White Mountains of New Hampshire in 1640 when he was sent out by Governor Winthrop to explore the territory north of the Massachusetts Bay Colony.

Driven by increasing economic and political pressures at home, and lured by the prospect of independence and even prosperity in the New World, as many as 100,000 Irish traveled to the North American colonies before 1700, and up to four times that number decided to try their luck across the ocean in the century that followed. Perhaps three-fourths of the immigrants before 1700 were Catholics, but during the next century many more Protestant Dissenters — especially Ulster Presbyterians — and even Anglicans swelled the exodus to North America.

A large number of the poorer emigrants came as indentured servants. In exchange for free passage and promises of some sort of recompense when they had fulfilled their obligation, they agreed to spend a specified number of years working for the master who paid their way across, fed and clothed them after they arrived, and sometimes taught them a trade. In the labor-hungry colonies, this arrangement was particularly advantageous for the prospective master, who could often get an indentured servant for an eighth the wages he would have had to pay a 'native born'. In 1678, a hundred Irish families who had indentured themselves in order to begin again in the New World arrived in Virginia and the Carolines from Barbados.

Other emigrants came as 'redemptioners', who were entitled to repay their passage when they landed if they could collect the money, sometimes from friends or family already living in the colonies. Wealthier merchants or farmers might recruit servants to go with them on the voyage. And a small number of emigrants paid their own fare — an amount equal to over a year's wages for the poor laborers and farmhands.

The trip across was not an easy one. Particularly during the seventeenth century, up to a third of the voyagers often perished, either during the passage or during the first year's 'seasoning'. In 1670 Virginia's governor reported that a full four-fifths of the indentured servants died soon after they arrived from disease, harsh weather or overwork. Conditions in the ship's hold, where poor passengers were confined, were cramped, overcrowded and unsanitary. Food and water onboard were generally inadequate, and many passengers, already weak and undernourished, succumbed to typhus, scurvy and other diseases.

Even if they survived the voyage over, these earliest immigrants often found their new land a difficult place to put down roots. They had come from a tightly knit society, where families worked their few acres together. Villagers in the *clachans,* the rural farming communities, traditionally shared implements and supplies and helped each other with building, sowing and harvesting. Families were close-knit and loyal, and family members felt a strong responsibility to share whatever they had with each other.

Colonial masters, however, did not always feel obligated to fulfill their part of even the written indenture agreement. Whereas in Ireland a wide array of unspoken obligations had been supported and maintained by tradition and public opinion, the colonial laws protecting servants were usually inadequate and were a poor defense against greedy masters with property and education on their side. One servant girl in Maryland wrote home that

> *I . . . am toiling almost day and night, . . . then tied up and whipped to that degree that you'd not serve an animal. [We have] scarce anything but Indian corn and salt to eat, and that even begrudged. Nay, many negroes are better used. [We are] almost naked, no shoes nor stockings to wear. And . . . after slaving during Master's pleasure, what rest we can get is to wrap ourselves in a blanket and lie upon the ground.*

She then begged her father, "if you have any bowels of compassion left," to send her some clothing. Colonial newspapers of the day carried many advertisements for Irish servants or apprentices who ran away to try to escape such conditions.

For those who managed to endure, however, and finish out their period of indenture, there was always the chance financial and social acceptance and success. As one emigrant wrote in a letter home in 1737: 'There is servants comes here out of

CHAPTER ONE

LEFT *The first Carrolls came to Maryland in 1688 and quickly became the most important Irish-Catholic family in the colonies. Charles Carroll, born in 1737, was the only Catholic to sign the Declaration of Independence. He was also the wealthiest and longest-lived of the signers; he died at age 95. This statue of Carroll stands in Statuary Hall in the United States Capitol.*

CHAPTER ONE

Ereland, who are now Justices of the Piece . . . .'

Most of those who came to the colonies as indentured servants were single men, but there were a number of single women as well. Few poor families could afford to make the trip together, although some families did travel from Ulster, often as part of whole congregations fleeing Anglican persecution. The single laborers were usually children of impoverished farmers or farmhands, although some were prisoners convicted of crimes — often acts of rebellion against the British — or even the victims of greedy merchants and shipmasters, who kidnapped and then transported their human cargo to America before auctioning them off as servants to the highest bidders. The young colonies' almost insatiable need for laborers unfortunately encouraged such unscrupulous practices.

Although most emigrants came from rural farming communities, lack of funds and the forbidding loneliness of the American frontier kept many from trying to begin again on the land. This letter home, written by an Irish farmer who had shaped a homestead from the Missouri wilderness, contrasts the life there with the one he had left:

> I could then go to a fair, or a wake, or a dance . . . I could spend the winter's nights in a neighbor's house cracking jokes by the turf fire. If I had there but a sore head I could have a neighbor within very hundred yards of me that would run to see me. But here everyone can get so much land . . . that they calls them neighbors that live two or three miles off.

For those who, like this man, decided to give farming a try, land was a bargain: an acre of fertile frontier terrain could be bought for the same amount it cost to rent an often overworked acre of farmland in Ireland. Virginia and Maryland were popular destinations, and areas named 'New Munster' and 'New Ireland' testified to the origin of their settlers. Anglo-Irish families such as the Butlers and the Lynches founded prosperous plantations along Chesapeake Bay and the coasts of the Carolinas. One well-known 'Irish Tract' ran through the Shenandoah Valley. Ulster Irish occupied Ulster County in New York's Mohawk Valley and carved our farms from the rich soil of Pennsylvania and New Jersey, gradually moving west and south into the frontier wilderness of Virginia, the Carolinas and Georgia. They wore fringed hunting shirts and moccasins, and built

themselves log cabins with earthen floors. But they also founded schools to train ministers for their Presbyterian churches — among them such universities as Princeton, Dickinson, Washington and Jefferson, Allegheny and Hampden-Sydney. The plantation economies of the West Indies also needed agricultural workers, but many of the Irish who settled — or were sent there by Cromwell — eventually made their way to the mainland. Merchants and tradesmen and their servants, on the other hand, swelled the populations of the large and growing towns along the eastern seaboard, such as New York, Philadelphia and Boston, where a bustling grade had grown up that exchanged Irish provisions and textiles for Chesapeake tobacco and West Indian sugar.

There were also a number of Irish from privileged families who saw the New World as a place to carve out an affluent way of life very much like the one they had left. These settlers were well-educated and relatively well off; a few were even members of the Anglo-Irish Ascendancy, the privileged alliance of Anglican churchmen, aristocrats, landed gentry and government officials, who departed with the promise of land and often titled positions in the New World. Sir Thomas Dongan, born in Kildare, was named governor of New York in 1682, for example, and Richard Kryle, described as 'an Irish gentleman', became governor of South Carolina in 1684. A large number of Irish followed him and settled there after his appointment. Charles O'Carroll of Tipperary, grandfather of a signer of the Declaration of Independence, was appointed Lord Baltimore's attorney general in Maryland and founded one of the most famous Irish-American families of the early South; it produced both a United States senator and the first Catholic bishop born in this country. And William Johnson, a native of Meath, settled

in the Mohawk Valley in northern New York, where he became a very substantial gentleman landowner and in 1755 was created a baronet. Later he served as the Crown's Superintendent of Indian Affairs for the region and, from his frontier mansion, exercised a commanding influence over the neighboring Mohawk Indians and the Irish tenant farmers he helped to emigrate and then put to work on his extensive holdings. By the time of his death, just before the outbreak of the American Revolution, Johnson had also served as a general and was a dominant force in frontier politics.

Wherever the new immigrants settled, they carried with them their traditions, their institutions, their sense of national identity and ties to the homeland. Most of those who made up the constant stream of new arrivals before the Revolution were by religion either Presbyterian of Scottish descent from the northern province of Ulster and other 'Dissenters', or members of the Anglican Church of Ireland. The Reverend Francis Makemie, from Donegal, often called the 'Father of American Presbyterianism', created the first American presbytery in Virginia in 1706 after spending more than 20 years as a wandering evangelist. A group of Irish Methodists founded the Methodist Church in America in 1768 — the Wesley Chapel on John Street in New York City.

Many Catholics found it difficult to practice their religion after they arrived and converted to one of these local churches. Although Catholics in Ireland made up between 75 and 80 percent of the population, the vitriolic English prejudice against 'popery' and stringent laws restricting the civil and religious liberties of Irish Catholics influenced the legislation of almost all the American colonies. Puritan New England, which was racially very homogeneous and between 85 and 90

percent Congregational, was particularly inhospitable. Laws taxing the import of Irish servants — aimed at excluding Catholics from the colony — were passed by the South Carolina legislature as early as 1698, and Maryland and Massachusetts enacted similar laws soon after to discourage Irish and Catholic settlers. A small Irish Catholic community did grow up, however, mainly in the tolerant Commonwealth of Pennsylvania, and there devout adherents reaffirmed their allegiance to the church that had been a source of support and community solidarity in the long struggle against oppressive English laws and landlords. The first public mass was held in Philadelphia in 1699, authorized by mayor James Logan of Armagh, who had come to the colony as secretary to William Penn. He later rose to become acting governor and then Chief Justice of the Commonwealth. The first Catholic parish was also formed here in 1733, and *The Pennsylvania Packet,* which in 1784 became the first daily newspaper in America, was founded in Philadelphia in 1771 by John Dunlap of County Tyrone.

The Irish community in Boston was also growing rapidly, and gained over 2,600 new residents in the three years before 1720. It was here in 1737 that the Charitable Irish Society was founded on St. Patrick's Day by 26 merchants, shipowners and other community leaders. The oldest Irish society in the United States, it was intended to 'aid unfortunate fellow countrymen, to cultivate a spirit of unity and harmony among all Irishmen in the Massachusetts colony and their descendants and to advance their interests socially and morally'.

The first recorded celebration of St. Patrick's Day in America took place in 1762 in New York, the third major city on the Atlantic seaboard to become home to a large Irish community. It was held at the house of John Marshall, near King's College — which later became Columbia University. Irishman Hugh Gaine's New York *Mercury* carried many stories about Irish merchants and schoolteachers in the burgeoning metropolis. There was even a Constable O'Sullivan, who may well have been one of the nation's first 'Irish cops', and who was killed in the line of duty in 1765.

Although they were a mere trickle compared with the stream of their countrymen who would set out to begin a new life in America in the years to come, the Irish who had made America their home on the eve of the Revolution were already abandoning the rural, agrarian life of their homeland for a totally new and different kind of existence in the young but rapidly expanding cities.

CHAPTER ONE

LEFT *The Carroll Mansion in Baltimore still stands as a monument to this prominent family. This leather-bound family Bible dates to 1654.*

ABOVE *Major General Henry Knox (1750–1806) began his career as a bookseller in Boston. He became George Washington's chief artillerist. The guns he placed around Boston led to the city's evacuation by the British on St. Patrick's Day, 1776. This engraving is flattering; Knox weighed 280 pounds.*

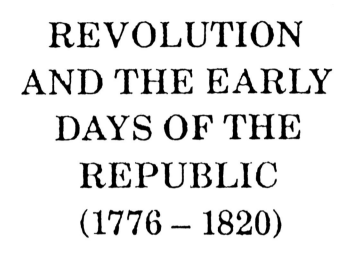

REVOLUTION AND THE EARLY DAYS OF THE REPUBLIC
(1776 – 1820)

CHAPTER TWO

On March 5, 1770, British troops fired on protesting natives in the streets of Boston, an event that American rebels were soon calling the 'Boston Massacre'. Among the five men killed that day was Patrick Carr, an Irishman. This event symbolized the sympathy many Irish, those still in the homeland as well as those who had emigrated, felt for the young Colonies' gathering revolt against their common enemy, the British.

Many who had already settled in the Colonies joined the Continental army and fought valiantly for the American cause, although others, particularly those who had been granted land and positions by the King, remained loyal to and fought for the Crown. One Loyalist regiment, Lord Rawdon's Volunteers of Ireland, performed so valiantly that it was incorporated into the regular British army after the war; in 1779 it organized the first New York St. Patrick's Day parade ever recorded. The Royal North Carolinians, another Irish regiment, served under Lord Cornwallis alongside regular British army recruits in the Carolinas campaign. Loyal Irish volunteers were also summoned to help defend Boston when General George Washington lay siege to it.

The majority of Americans of Irish heritage, however, felt strong sympathy for the radicals in their fight for independence, and a number distinguished themselves as officers under General Washington. As many as one-third to one-half the colonial troops were probably either born in Ireland or had Irish parents, including 1,492 officers and 26 generals, of whom 15 were Irish-born. General Sir Henry Clinton summed up the fervor of the Irish patriots when he declared that "the emigrants from Ireland are in general . . . our most serious antogonists".

Among the many noted Irish officers was John Sullivan, whose father had emigrated from Limerick in 1723. Sullivan was hailed as 'the first to take up arms against the King' after he led New Hampshire militiamen in an attack on Fort William and Mary in Newcastle, New Hampshire, in 1774. The gunpowder they captured there was later used at the Battle of Bunker Hill. Sullivan was a major-general in the Continental Army and later, in 1779, he defeated the alliance of the Iroquois and Loyalists in New York State. General Richard Montgomery, a native of Dublin, invaded Canada and captured Montreal before being killed in an attack on Quebec City in December 1775. Another officer of Irish birth, Andrew Lewis, had actually served as a colonel in the British

army before joining the patriots in 1776 as a brigadier general. While in the service of the British he had defeated the Shawnee Indians at Point Pleasant, a strategically important spot on the Ohio River, thus opening up the Northwest Territory to American penetration after the outbreak of the Revolution. Irish sharpshooter Timothy Murphy of Morgan's Rifle Corps was the son of immigrants and was to become the most famous marksman of the Revolution. He put the colonists a large step closer to victory when he killed two British commanders during the Battle of Saratoga. Even George Washington's most important 'confidential agent' was an Irish-born tailor named Hercules Mulligan. By serving as a double agent while the British occupied New York, Mulligan was able to gather much valuable inform-

IN MEMORY OF

ANDREW JACKSON,

The Illustrious

PATRIOT,

Statesman and Hero.

DIED JUNE 8TH 1845.

ÆT. 78.

ation on enemy strategy for the Patriot cause.

It was not just on land that Irish warriors distinguished themselves during the American fight for independence. Many fought valiantly for the cause at sea. Jeremiah O'Brien, whose father came from Cork, captured the British schooner *Margaretta* off the coast of Maine on June 12, 1775, in the first naval battle of the Revolution. Another Irish-American revolutionary hero, Wexford-born John Barry, became the 'Father of the United States Navy' when he was commissioned its commodore in February 1797, after outstanding service during the War of Independence.

The valor of the many Irish enlisted men in the Continental army was also crucial to the success of the American cause. Among them was Andrew Jackson, the son of immigrants from County

Antrim, who was later elected President of the young republic. After seeing duty as a soldier during the Revolution, Jackson went on to fight the British a second time during the War of 1812, when he won a major victory as commander at the Battle of New Orleans. He is honored by the American Irish as a great soldier, leader, and friend of the common man.

On the day the British evacuated Boston — March 17, 1776 — General Washington acknowledged the invaluable support of his many Irish officers and men by designating 'St. Patrick' the

CHAPTER TWO

RIGHT *Politics and the Irish have always gone together. John Ferguson was Mayor of New York City in 1815.*

RIGHT CENTER *The White House, seen from the North Lawn. It was modeled by architect James Hoban after Leinster House in Dublin, meeting place of the Irish Parliament.*

password of the day. Soon after, on July 4, 1776, the break with England became irrevocable when members of the Continental Congress signed the Declaration of Independence. Three native-born Irish were among the signers — Dubliner James Smith, a lawyer, redemptioner George Taylor, both of Pennsylvania; and Matthew Thornton of New Hampshire, a physician, who had emigrated with his parents when he was three. Signers of Irish descent included Charles Carroll, the only Catholic (whose family had dropped the initial 'O' from their name), Thomas Lynch, Thomas McKean, George Read and Edward Rutledge. The Secretary of the Continental Congress, Charles Thomson, whose duty it was to read the Declaration to that body for the first time, was also Irish-born. After his parents died, Thomson left Derry as an indentured servant at the age of 10, and rose in less than 20 years to become a well-to-do merchant in the thriving commercial city of Philadelphia.

In addition, the printer to Congress who printed the document, John Dunlap, had come to America from County Tyrone in 1757; in 1771 he founded *The Pennsylvania Packet*. A weekly when it first began publication, *The Packet* later became the first daily newspaper to be published in the new United States.

Many Irish, both at home and in the Colonies, applauded the American revolt as a struggle against their common enemy, the British. Dunlap's paper reflected this feeling in an attack on the Loyalists that he published on August 5, 1779:

Who were the occasion of this war? The Tories! . . . Who advised and who assisted in burning your towns, ravaging your country, and violating the chastity of your women? . . . Who have always counteracted the endeavors of Congress to secure the liberties of this country? . . . In short, who wish to see us conquered, to see us slaves? The Tories!

Awake, Americans, to a sense of your danger . . . Instantly banish every Tory from among you. Let America be sacred only to freemen. Drive far from you every baneful wretch who wishes to see you fettered with the chains of tyranny.

Meanwhile, the war made emigration from Ireland even more difficult than before. Enemy warships were always a threat to travelers on the long journey across the Atlantic, and ships of the British Navy often stopped passenger vessels in mid-voyage and empressed those aboard into the Crown's undermanned forces. In response to such hazards, and despite a drop in the linen trade and ever-rising rents in Ireland, the steady flow of emigrants to America — as many as 30,000

CHAPTER TWO

LEFT *William McKinley, 25th President of the United States, was born in Ohio in 1843. After a career in Congress he became President in 1897 and was re-elected in 1900. This photo dates from 1898. McKinley was president during the Spanish-American War, from which the United States emerged as a world power. He was assassinated in 1901.*

Ulster natives had fled during the five years before the war — fell off. It was not until 1783 and the end of hostilities that it would pick up again.

While the fighting continued, however, Irish pioneers in North America were moving westward and helping to push back the frontiers of their adopted homeland. Daniel Boone and others of Irish descent explored the wilderness of Kentucky and built homes there, and Irish settlers continued to surge west and south into the Ohio Valley and the back country of Georgia and the Carolinas. During the 1780s the repeal of discriminatory colonial laws made the young United States an even more appealing haven to Catholics, who despite the partial revocation of the oppressive Penal Laws in the 1790s continued to suffer legal repression in Ireland for another 50 years. Although Irish Catholics would not emigrate in large numbers until well into the next century, when the first U.S. census was taken in 1790 it recorded 44,000 Irish-born residents out of a total population of 3,000,000 — over half of them in the states south of Pennsylvania. Some historians believe there were actually two or three times that number. Approximately 150,000 citizens of Irish ancestry were also living in the new nation at that time.

With the British surrender at Yorktown, five years after the Colonies had declared their independence, the American Revolution triumphed and Irish supporters of the American cause congratulated General Washington on his victory.

The nationalist movement in Ireland had become more active as economic and social conditions worsened, and in a letter to the Yankee Club of Stewartstown, County Tyrone, Washington asserted that

> *The generous indignation, against the foes to the rights of human nature, with which you seem to be animated, and the exalted sentiments of liberty, which you appear to entertain, are too consonant to the feelings and principles of the citizens of the United States of America, not to attract their veneration and esteem . . . If in the course of our successful contest, any good consequence have resulted to the oppressed kingdom of Ireland, it will afford a new source of felicitation to all who respect the interests of humanity.*

One such 'good consequence' was a direct result of British preoccupation with the war in America and the agitation of such Yankee clubs who, inspired by the American example, organized conventions or 'congresses', boycotted English products and threatened revolution if the British

CHAPTER TWO

RIGHT *General Richard Montgomery defeated the French army in Canada in 1760, ending the French and Indian War. The war lost the French their control of Canada and the routes west, and led to increased emigration from England and Ireland.*

government did not meet their demands. Among the most famous Irish Patriot leaders of this struggle were Henry Grattan and Charles Lucas. In 1782 Westminster bowed to their pressure and granted Ireland the right to legislate her own domestic affairs by creating an Irish Parliament. In response to this 'revolution of 1782', Grattan happily claimed that 'the American war was the Irish harvest'.

At the same time, the end of hostilities between Britain and America unleashed a flood of new emigrants from Irish shores — perhaps as many as 150,000 left between 1783 and 1814. The trade in Irish servants declined because captains of British ships could no longer be certain American courts would uphold contracts of indenture. Members of the Ascendancy feared a drain of skilled workers, however — enough to pass legislation making it illegal to 'contract with, entice, persuade, solicit or seduce any manufacturer, workman, or artificer' to leave the country. An even more stringent Passenger Act of 1803 set up tougher requirements regarding the number of passengers a ship could carry and the amount of provisions they had to bring with them. By effectively raising fares far beyond the means of the poor, the Act ensured that only the fairly well-to-do could emigrate. As a result, most of those who left Ireland for America during this period were successful farmers, skilled craftsmen, or businessmen and professionals — merchants, clerks, schoolmasters, doctors, and their families.

To help these growing numbers of immigrants adjust to life in their new country, some of the more affluent and established Irish-American residents created organizations such as the Charitable Irish Society in Boston and the Society for the Relief of Emigrants from Ireland, which was begun in Philadelphia in 1793 — the favorite port of entry and the same city whose flourishing Irish community had started a Hibernian Society in 1790. Among the founders of the former was Matthew Carey, a prominent publisher, bookseller, and intellectual leader, who had been a noted newspaper editor in Dublin before escaping to America to avoid prosecution for speaking out against the Crown. A Benevolent Hibernian Society was founded in Baltimore in 1803, and in 1814 New York's Irish community created its own Irish Emigrant Society to protect and assist new arrivals.

Even as Irish-Americans in the United States were organizing to welcome and assist their newly arrived fellow countrymen, however, the government of the new nation was taking steps to restrict and regulate the influx of immigrants. After the French Revolution and the 1798 United Irish uprising, many political refugees sought asylum in America. Fearing the spread of extremist ideas, which might abet the domestic republicanism of radical representatives such as County Wicklow–born Matthew Lyon of Vermont, the American Federalist Party passed laws that extended the required residence period for citizenship from five to fourteen years and gave the President the right to expel 'dangerous' aliens by executive decree. "If some means are not adopted," insisted Massachusetts Congressman Harrison Gray Otis in 1797, "to prevent the indiscriminate admission of wild Irishmen and others to the right of suffrage, there will . . . be an end to liberty and property." A third such law, called the Sedition Act, declared it a misdemeanor to make statements 'with the intent to defame' Congress and the President, or statements that might bring them into 'contempt or disrepute'. Lyon, an ardent admirer of Jefferson and the French Revolution, was the first to be prosecuted.

Among those who emigrated at this time was James McKinley of County Antrim, grandfather of President William McKinley, who left after his brother Francis was hanged as a United Irish rebel. Many rebel leaders fled as well to escape prosecution and execution for treason, including Thomas Addis Emmet, older brother of condemned revolutionary Robert Emmet, who was hanged by the British for his defiant nationalism after he led an unsuccessful rebellion in 1803. The courageous speech he delivered at his trial made him a popular hero on both sides of the Atlantic. The elder Emmet, who had helped found the Society of United Irishmen, was admitted to the New York Bar by a special legislative act. It was the first step in a brilliant political career in New York State, where he eventually served as attorney general. Theobald Wolfe Tone, originator of the concept of violent separatist revolution still advocated by many Irish nationalists, also spent a period of exile in America before returning to arrange for the landing of a French invasion force that was to aid the Irish separatists. He was captured and committed suicide while in prison after his request for an honorable execution before a firing squad was denied.

Many of these exiles — predominantly Protestant, middle-class professionals — became leaders of the Irish-American communities where they settled and were widely respected and admired. One, Patrick Rogers, was the father of William Barton Rogers, first president of the Massachusetts Institute of Technology. Another distinguished exile of '98 was William Macneven, president of the Irish Emigrant Society and author of *Advice to Irishmen Arriving in America,* as well as a noted professor of obstetrics at the College of Physicians and Surgeons. Robert Patterson, who also left Ireland after the revolt, later became director of the federal mint.

While the failure of the 1798 uprising sent many of its key figures abroad, some members of the ruling Ascendancy at home in Ireland, fearing continued popular unrest, supported passage of the 1801 Act of Union, by which the Irish Parliament voted itself out of existence and created instead a United Kingdom of Great Britain and Ireland. Many Irish Catholics also welcomed the Act of Union because British Prime Minister Pitt promised Catholic emancipation in its wake, but the Act later became a major target of Irish nationalists and their American Irish supporters.

In the new American republic, however, massive Irish-American support helped assure the election of Thomas Jefferson in 1800 and the defeat of the conservative Federalists, led by Alexander Hamilton. Jefferson's concept of a broadly based popular democracy was more consonant with the ideals of the United Irish rebellion, and its leaders heartily embraced his presidency. Among his staunch supporters was William Duane, an Irish-born newspaperman and graduate of Trinity College, Dublin. Under his editorship *The Aurora,* a Philadelphia newspaper, be-

CHAPTER TWO

LEFT *John Marshall, perhaps the greatest Chief Justice of the United States Supreme Court, was born in Virginia in 1755. He was appointed to the Supreme Court in 1801 and served until 1835.*

came one of the primary vehicles for Jefferson's republican sentiments.

The expanding economy and social tolerance of Jeffersonian America soon made it possible for skilled and enterprising Irish immigrants to achieve a degree of material comfort and even prosperity that would have been impossible in the strife-torn and repressive land of their birth. The young nation was just embarking on a period of rapid and dynamic economic expansion, and it needed and rewarded those who were willing to work.

The Penal Laws of the eighteenth century had barred Catholics in Ireland from entering the professions and skilled trades. As a result the majority of Irish immigrants, particularly those raised in southern Ireland, came from a rural, agricultural background. They were not prepared to take up life in the burgeoning cities of their new homeland. So to help find jobs for the many who left after the 1812–15 war, the Irish Emigrant Society in 1816 opened a new office on Nassau Street in New York City.

The following year it took a much bolder step, however, and asked Congress to set aside a portion of Illinois for the new arrivals, who would be allowed to buy the land on 14 years credit and who would 'serve as a frontier guard against marauding Indians'. The House of Representatives voted to reject the proposal by an 83 to 71 margin, however, and by that single act determined the direction of Irish-American history for well over a century to come: despite their agrarian upbringing, the American Irish would henceforth be an urban people.

ABOVE *A ragged Irishman considers emigrating to America in*
this lithograph from 1854. Cheap fares and relatively swift
and safe ships contributed to increased immigration.

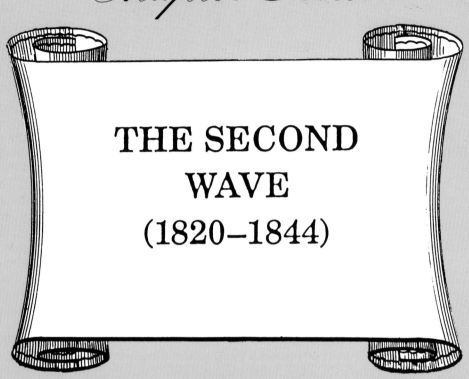

THE SECOND
WAVE
(1820–1844)

CHAPTER THREE

BELOW RIGHT *The masthead of* The Shamrock *in 1812. The first important Irish newspaper in New York,* The Shamrock *was founded by Thomas O'Conor in 1810; publication ceased in 1816.*

*I*t was in the burgeoning cities of the new republic that Irish-Americans enjoyed their first important political and social successes. As early as 1784 James Duane, a former member of the Continental Congress, had been elected the first post-colonial mayor of New York; Massachusetts picked James Sullivan, son of a Limerick native, to be its governor in 1808. His brother, Major General Sullivan, was the famed conqueror of the Iroquois. *The Shamrock,* the first Irish-American newspaper, also began in New York in 1810. Its editor was United Irish refugee Thomas O'Connor, who later became a key figure in the Tammany Hall political organization.

Individual Irish Catholics also triumphed socially in this interval before the 1830s swell of immigration, managing to achieve a degree of sucess in 'high society' that would not be repeated for at least a century. The daughter of Charles Carroll, Mrs. Richard Caton, set the tone for American society and as its premier unofficial social arbiter made While Sulphur Springs the original fashionable resort. Her three daughters were also the first American heiresses to marry into the British nobility, becoming respectively the Marchioness of Wellesley, the Duchess of Leeds and the Baroness Stafford. The English called them 'the American Graces'.

In New York it was Dominick Lynch who led fashionable society. Educated in Ireland and France by an Irish father who had brought a large fortune with him when he emigrated after the American Revolution, Lynch was a gourmet and wine importer who introduced a number of fine French wines to American tables, including the highly prized Château Margaux. He also helped introduce grand opera to the United States by mounting the first American production of *The Barber of Seville* in November 1826. Lynch's New York townhouse and Westchester County estate were the scenes of stylish social gatherings and musical events, where Lynch himself often sang.

The lifestyle of these Irish-American aristocrats differed starkly, however, from that of the thousands of Irish who would settle in American cities after the close of the War of 1812 made the seas safe again. Besides Andrew Jackson, a number of other noted Irish-American officers helped America emerge triumphant in that conflict with England. Commodore Richard Macdonough commanded the American naval forces on Lake Champlain, closing off a possible invasion from Canada when he vanquished the British at Plattsburg; in the Mediterranean, Commodore John Shaw led the United States Naval Squadron.

The end of the war in 1815 coincided with economic recession in England and Ireland, continued farm evictions and the enclosure of farms to make room for sheep grazing. Rents rose as the available land shrank; by 1841 close to 80 percent of Ireland's potential farmland was under grass. When industrialization closed off home spinning and weaving as sources of supplementary income, many families had to cut back severely on their already skimpy diets to pay their keep, often subsisting on nothing but potatoes and drippings. At the same time, Ireland was in the midst of a population explosion that sent its numbers soaring from about three million to over eight million between 1725 and 1841. The already tiny (averaging around five acres) and overworked Irish farms

THE SHAMROCK;
OR,
HIBERNIAN CHRONICLE.

"FOSTERED UNDER THY WING, WE DIE IN THY DEFENCE."

VOL. II.   NEW-YORK, SATURDAY, MAY 23, 1812.   NO. 24—WHOLE NO. 76.

For the moon never beams without bringing me dreams
Of the beautiful Annabel Lee;
And the stars never rise but I see the bright eyes
Of the beautiful Annabel Lee;
And so, all the night-tide, I lie down by the side
Of my darling, my darling, my life and my bride
In her sepulchre there by the sea —
In her tomb by the side of the sea.

were subdivided even further by fathers trying to provide for all their sons; the sons found it even harder to wrest a living from the ever-smaller patches of land. If a father decided to keep his farm intact, however, so that it would provide a decent living for the son who inherited it, the other sons often had no choice but to seek their fortune in England or America. With no land to work, these young men could not marry; many young Irish girls also emigrated to find bride-grooms with better prospects. Still other emi-grants fled from the civil strife that festered for years as landlord-tenant relations steadily de-teriorated and Catholic terrorist bands like the Terry Alts and the Ribbonmen fought landlords and their representatives, guerrilla-style, with night-time raids and killings. At one point mur-ders had become so common that a coroner de-clared an assassinated land agent had died of 'natural causes'. Frequent food shortages, starva-tion and epidemics also resulted from local or island-wide failures of the potato crop — which occurred in eight out of ten years during the

1830s—and convinced many farmers, both Catho-lics and Protestants, that the time had finally come to emigrate.

The vibrant American economy described in letters home from earlier immigrants had a strong appeal to people who had endured such trials, and they began to dream of an American Eden overflowing with milk and honey. Soldiers returning from the war of 1812–15 spread the word that game in North America was so plenti-ful that "all a man wanted was a gun and . . . ammunition to be able to live like a prince," and the Irish poet Pádraig Cúndún reported that he owned "outright a fine farm of land" in upstate New York where "my family and I can eat our fill of bread and meat, butter and milk any day we like throughout the year . . ." As early as 1818 John Doyle wrote home from New York City re-commending his adopted nation to any "enterpris-ing man, desirous of advancing himself in the world" and picturing it as a "free country, where a man is allowed to thrive and flourish without having a penny taken by government."

The steady economic growth that inspired such letters led to increased trade between Britain and her former colonies, which by the 1830s put a transatlantic voyage within the means of even the less well-off Irish, such as laborers and servants. In 1836, in fact, these groups made up almost 60 percent of the Irish arriving in New York. Many who would have taken advantage of cheaper fares by sailing first to Quebec and other Canadian ports of entry could now embark directly for the States, and this route became even more popular after steamships began carrying passengers from Ireland to Liverpool in the 1820s. There would-be emigrants to America could book passage on more reliable vessels with more dependable schedules than those sailing from the smaller Irish ports. And because so many of the ships that left Liverpool transported their cargo of British manufactured goods directly to New York, the Empire City soon became the main port of entry for Irish immigrants and the burgeoning Irish-American capital of the United States.

Many of the new arrivals still had relatives in Ireland who wanted to 'come out to America', and so they saved until they could send enough dollars home from their often meager earnings to pay for a brother's or a sister's or a cousin's fare across. In 1838 over half the Irish who arrived came on tickets purchased by Irish-American friends or relatives, and by the 1840s more than $1 million a year was being sent back to bring others over or to help out those who remained.

Although travel conditions had improved greatly since the eighteenth century, the voyage from Ireland to America was still a hard one. Technical refinements cut the average crossing time from eight or ten weeks to only five or six by 1830, and from that year on most vessels were specifically built for passengers rather than cargo. In addition, both the British and the American governments tried to regulate the traffic to protect travelers from abuses. Britain passed a series of Passenger Acts to this end between 1803 and 1842, but they proved generally ineffective. Emigrants usually had to negotiate the many pains and pitfalls of the long journey with little or no help.

The first leg of the trip, from various Irish ports to Liverpool (or sometimes Greenock, in Scotland), took anywhere from 14 to 30 hours, but they were often hours spent standing, jammed between baggage and livestock, on open decks — where one captain admitted to crowding in over 1,400 passengers. Even the Irish who came from coastal areas were usually unaccustomed to being on board a ship, and it was a new and terrifying experience

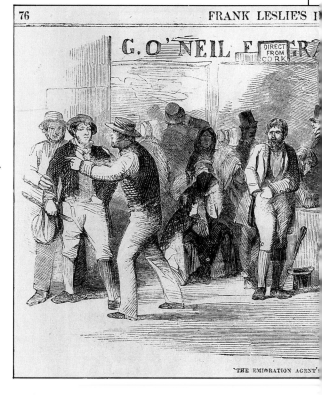

76   FRANK LESLIE'S I

'THE EMIGRATION AGENT'

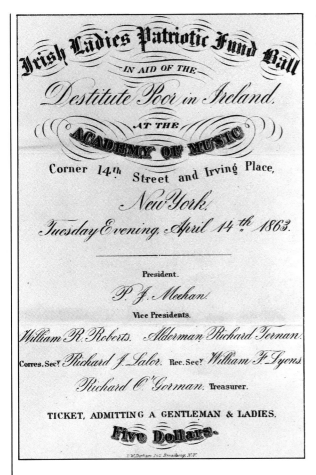

PASSAGE MONEY PAID.

CHAPTER THREE

LEFT *Well-to-do Irish-Americans organized fundraising social events to aid the Irish poor. Funds from America contributed significantly to a rising standard of living among Irish farmers during the late nineteenth century.*

BELOW LEFT *Entire families emigrated together to the United States. In this woodcut, which appeared in* Frank Leslie's Illustrated Newspaper *in 1856, outbound passengers gather in the emigration agent's office. These agents were often unscrupulous and fleeced the emigrants.*

for many. Passengers clung to each other or whatever was handy to keep from being washed overboard when the weather got rough, and seasickness was almost universal.

After they disembarked at Liverpool, though, the new arrivals had even worse trials awaiting them. There they had to negotiate an entire array of ticket agents, passage agents, roominghouse keepers, porters and others who took full advantage of the passengers' naiveté to defraud them of the funds and provisions they had brought with them for the long journey and their new life.

The first priority, of course, was to buy a ticket for passage. But this often turned out to be either completely worthless or for travel on an old and less-than-seaworthy ship that was sailing to a port far from the emigrant's destination. Eager ticket vendors often lied about the actual departure date, leaving many people at the mercy of rapacious boardinghouse owners and saloon-keepers while they waited weeks or even months to put to sea. Captains were much less interested in the health of their passengers once the trade in indentured servants declined, and after about 1800 most travelers had to pack and prepare their own provisions. Some captains earned tidy sums by intentionally underestimating the length of the voyage so that passengers would be forced to purchase food onboard at very inflated prices when their own supplies ran out.

When the long-awaited day of departure finally arrived, passengers often had only a few minutes to board between the loading of cargo and the moment the tide was right to cast off. In the headlong scramble people were pushed, pulled and even thrown in head-first over the sides of the ship, and their baggage tossed in on top of them.

Once at sea, captains often proved drunken or inept, crews inadequate or incompetent, and ships so leaky that they had to be pumped out by both passengers and seamen to keep them afloat. In steerage, up to 700 were crowded in and forced to sleep four travelers to a bunk. One wrote that "It would be well for everyone to remember that all the room that a passenger can claim for himself is about two and a half feet in height, two feet wide, and six feet along, and in this small space he eats, lives, sleeps, etc. When it is mealtime, the steward comes past each man and gives everyone his share in his tin, in bed. It is the nearest thing in the world to feeding time at [an] animal show".

When a storm blew up, the hatches were battened down and passengers were confined below with no light and very little air. Few escaped the agonies of seasickness, but unsanitary conditions

CHAPTER THREE

RIGHT *Immigrants to America from Ireland usually left from Queenstown. This engraving appeared in* Harper's Weekly *in May 1874.*

also bred disease; required medical exams before boarding were cursory at best, and it was a rare ship indeed that carried a doctor. There were shipboard epidemics of typhus in 1817–18 and cholera in the 1830s, and dysentery was a common complaint of passengers forced to eat spoiled food and drink contaminated water. Cramped, homesick and seasick, terrified when blown about by a sudden gale and bored when the weather was calm, passengers were more than thankful to finally reach their destination.

When they did disembark in America, though, usually in one of the big ports like Boston, New York or Philadelphia, a whole new array of swindlers and con men awaited them. Once again they had to negotiate the crowd of baggage-handlers, roominghouse owners, agents selling tickets for domestic travel, and even a few cunning ex-countrymen eager to share a cup of grog or porter and then fleece them of any remaining funds. Some arrived destitute — or had their money and baggage snatched by boardinghouse 'runners' — and spent their first night, and sometimes many more, sleeping in the streets that lined the harbor, just yards from where they had landed. An immigrant who landed in New York in 1833 described the disheartening scene:

> *It was half-past ten before we arrived at the quay. Here we were landed in the dark, the rain pouring upon us, and our luggage strewed all around. The shops . . . were all shut, and we had no one to direct us where to proceed. We had therefore no alternative than to pass the night where we were, in the open air . . . I constructed a barricade of the trunks belonging to myself and two fellow-passengers . . . over which I put some [planks] which were lying on the wharf. Under the lee of this shed, we placed the female passenger who was ill of a fever; and having procured a pitcher I proceeded into the town in search of water, and some wine for the woman. This I procured from a shop which I found still open, together with a bottle of brandy and some cheese. Myriads of rats kept squeaking and frisking about and over us all night; one of them captured a piece of cheese from my knee while I was at supper.*

When he went into town to look for a room the following day,

> *I passed two other encampments of immigrants in Washington Street. Some of them*

> *were lying huddled together under carts, some within the recesses of doors, and some on the bare pavement. I enquired at a good-looking elderly woman who was lying on the pavement — her head bare, and her long grey hair fluttering in the breeze — how long it was since she landed. She answered . . . that it was six nights, and that her party had lain all that time in the streets.*

When the immigrants finally found shelter, they were often crowded into noisy, dirty boardinghouses where they slept six or eight to a room. The lucky ones were met by friends or relatives, who might arrange lodging for the newcomers or help them get a job at the same mill or on the same construction project where they worked.

The small towns of America were fast becoming cities, and the cities were exploding into major metropolises. As one newspaper observed, 'America demands for her development an inexhaustible fund of physical energy, and Ireland supplies the most part of it. There are several sorts of power working at the fabric of this Republic — waterpower, steam-power, and Irish-power. The last works hardest of all.' The Irish landed on the shores of their new homeland and quickly set about building its roads and bridges, erecting its homes and offices, producing its textiles and its steel. They were the porters, the hod-carriers, the longshoremen, the wagon drivers, the housemaids and cooks and waitresses, the policemen and firemen. They took the toughest, most dangerous jobs, wherever they were to be had, for whatever pay they could get.

So the new Irish-Americans made the initial,

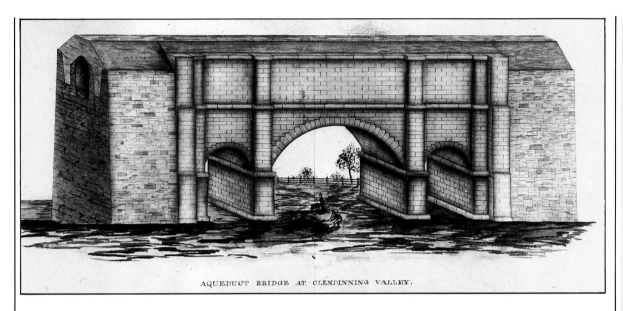

AQUEDUCT BRIDGE AT CLENDINNING VALLEY.

CHAPTER THREE

LEFT *Irish immigrants were often employed on massive construction projects. The Glendinning Valley aqueduct bridge in New York State was completed almost exclusively by Irish laborers in 1842.*

BELOW LEFT *The Irish section of New Orleans, a city with an important Irish population, was known as Irish Channel. This view was taken in 1947.*

painful transition to life in a new land, finding a job, settling in neighborhoods near friends and relatives from their old village whenever they could. Those who had come before held Saturday-night 'kitchen rackets' to welcome the 'greenhorns', stateside equivalents of the all-night 'American wakes' where they had said goodbye to friends and family before leaving Ireland. Soon a number of cities had their own large and growing Irish communities, among them New Orlean's waterfront 'Irish Channel', South Boston, Philadelphia's Kensington and Five Points in lower New York City. By 1833, in fact, New York City alone had an estimated 40,000 Irish-born residents. These Irish communities were for decades tightly knit, loyal neighborhoods that recreated and preserved the values of the homeland.

At some point, either on the voyage or after landing in the teeming streets of the New World, the disoriented immigrant began to realize that the standards of the Irish village he or she had left so recently were not the standards of the society they were about to enter. Catholics especially criticized the competitive, aggressive materialism and slick dishonesty that characterized the new republic, and contrasted so sharply with the familiar village lifestyle of family and neighborly solidarity, sharing and respect for spiritual and communal obligations. An Irish schoolmaster in Pennsylvania summed it up when he urged that 'we should be content with a moderate share of the wealth of the world' and should 'not be led away by avarice . . . in the pursuit of shadows or of filthy trash'. Even the most well-prepared immigrants often found the clash of values confusing and disorienting. Becoming an American

CHAPTER THREE

meant creating a completely new identity out of principles and ways of doing things they did not understand or believe in. This was to become a source of serious conflict with their Yankee neighbors before many more years went by.

But the Irish soon developed their own unique institutions that helped nurture and maintain traditional values, and in so doing strengthened even further their developing sense of ethnic identity and pride. The first of these institutions was the home itself. Often it was just a tenement or shanty where an entire family lived in a single room, but here the children were born and raised, meals were eaten, and neighbors dropped by to chat and gossip. This warm, open and communal style of living guaranteed that no emotions were hidden and no secrets could be kept, and it nurtured strong neighborhood and family loyalties.

The saloon, or *shebeen*, was another important center of Irish-American community life. Even if the Irish did not invent whiskey, which they called *uisque baugh* ('water of life'), the name at least conveyed their affection for the revered brew. In Ireland the pub was a fixture of village life, and the making and selling of illegal *poitín* had been a rare source of desperately needed revenue. Now in the new homeland illegal pubs were one of the few small businesses many Catholics could afford to start — a board, two barrels and a bottle were all that was required to set up shop. Among the rules the aspiring saloon keeper learned to follow if he (or she) wanted business to prosper were the following:

- *Never hire relatives, and don't trust the ones your wife makes you hire.*
- *When you're closed, you're closed. Everybody out.*
- *When women ask, say "He's not here."*
- *Always treat a priest.*
- *Don't let women stand at the bar [before the 1920s].*
- *Cash checks quietly, and don't trust a drinker.*
- *Don't fight with cops. Pay them.*

The heavily Irish neighborhoods of lower Manhattan alone had over 2,000 saloons by 1840, and a decade later Boston's mayor reported that two-thirds of that city's grog shops were Irish-owned. Irish workingmen, faced with 12 or 14 hours of backbreaking labor by day and crowded into ramshackle tenements by night, found the local pub a source of comfort and conviviality. Because the Irish continued to marry late, many single young men passed their time there, too,

alternately celebrating and denouncing their celibate state.

The saloons served several other purposes in the community. In an era without employment agencies, they were important referral sources for immigrants seeking work. They also functioned as centers of political effort and initiative, where local party candidates and causes were promoted, labor unionists could meet safely and Irish nationalist groups were welcome. Sports enthusiasts often gathered there, and even those involved in illegal sports like horse-racing, cock-fighting and prize-fighting could find a sympathetic ear where their gregarious neighbors met to drink, talk and tell tales. Despite Father Theobald Matthew's arrival from Ireland in the 1840s to preach success through abstinence (after urging that 'Ireland sober is Ireland free'), the saloon remained an important center of community life and enjoyed a heyday during the Gilded Era of the late nineteenth century.

The Catholic Church was the third important

institution that united the immigrant communities. The Church had supported the Irish when they were farmers struggling against their landlords and the Ascendancy, and it continued to support them as they struggled to gain a foothold in their adopted land. In return, grateful members contributed small amounts over the years until they could raise their first house of worship, and sometimes a school and parish house as well. These were often squat, graceless, red-brick buildings, but they were monuments nonetheless to the community's shared vision and solidarity. The religious majority that had been forced to attend mass secretly — often in the open fields — in Ireland now proudly declared its faith, with brick and mortar, as a religious minority in America.

Between 1789 and 1860, the Catholic Church in the United States grew from 30,000 parishioners under one bishop and served by 30 priests to a total of nearly 3 million members by 1850. Because many of the new faithful were Irish, they felt little sympathy with the aristocratic French clerics who dominated the American church, and they demanded Irish priests instead. Recalling the tactics of their oppressors in the old country, they also distrusted the religious education provided in the public schools via the King James version of the Bible, and insisted that they should receive state aid for their own church schools. An activist Irish clergy backed up their demands. The school question was a source of intense and very emotional conflict in New York

State during the 1830s and 40s, and ended in the secularization of the public schools by a vote of the state legislature in 1842. The ballot set an important precedent that ultimately resulted in the adoption of the principle of separation of church and state in tax-supported schools and colleges.

All three of these key elements in the developing Irish-American way of life — the tightly knit, crowded and lively homes and neighborhoods, the local saloons and the energetic, practical and sometimes parochial Catholic Church — were alien to the Anglo-Saxon, Yankee culture that had developed in the United States by the time large numbers of Irish began to arrive. That the newcomers were landing in such large numbers during the second quarter of the nineteenth century only made them stand out more. Over 50,000 Irish entered the U.S. between 1820 and 1830, and more than four times as many joined them during the decade that followed; by 1840 one out of every two U.S. immigrants was Irish. Between 1838 and 1844 alone more than 200,000 made the westward voyage, putting the total number of immigrants from Ireland since 1815 at over a million — a massive number of new residents for a young country like the United States, whose population in 1830 was not even 13 million!

The tendency of the gregarious, novelty-loving Irish to settle primarily in cities made them even more conspicuous. Most Americans in 1830 were farmers; only 10 percent of the population lived in urban areas. Even those who did, though, were frightened and confused by the rapid expansion of their hometowns during the early part of the century, and they blamed the Irish for the new problems of crime, noise, pollution and competition for jobs that accompanied this growth. What they saw of conditions in the 'Paddy Towns' and 'Little Dublins' shocked and horrified them. They regarded the hardworking, sociable, devout Irish as rough, crude, boisterous, superstitious and much too fond of the bottle. Thus the very communities the Irish saw as havens in a hostile, competitive new world were themselves fast becoming a major source of tension and conflict. By not just insulating but also isolating the Irish, these enclaves underlined the ways Irish-American attitudes, beliefs and lifestyles differed from those of their neighbors. And as Charles O'Conor, son of an exiled United Irishman, wrote, "This is an English colony, and its people inherit from their ancestors a . . . contempt for everything Irish." The Irish were truly urban pioneers, blazing a trail and shaping a new ghetto lifestyle for the Jewish, Italian and other immigrant groups who followed them to the cities of America. But as the first to drive a wedge into the self-satisfied homogeneity of nineteenth-century America, they also were the first to suffer the discrimination nativists reserved for those so clearly different from themselves.

If the Irish threatened America's perception of itself as a nation of farmers, however, they also seemed to threaten its staunchly Protestant underpinnings. Beginning with the Puritans, American culture shared the British dislike and distrust of 'popery', and most of the small minority of American Catholics practiced their religion discreetly. The Irish, however, were anything but discreet about their faith. Soon Protestant propagandists began to attack the 'foreign' religion and spread wild rumors. During the 1830s, for example, a majority of Americans probably believed that European despots were conspiring with the Church and its agents to overthrow the American democracy. Even such respected men as Lyman Beecher and Samuel F.B. Morse, the inventor of the telegraph, endorsed the reports. One publication stated that 'the Roman Catholic Church is the most dangerous enemy that the Republic has to encounter, and those . . . within its pale are the most dangerous enemies of the country'. In 1842, the newly formed American Protestant Association declared that Catholicism was 'in its principles and tendency, subversive of civil and religious liberty, and destructive to the spiritual welfare of men'. By 1835, as one observer noted, the writing and publishing of such anti-Catholic propaganda had 'become a part of the regular industry of the country, as much as the making of nutmegs or the construction of clocks'.

The most scandalous attack, however, was a literary hoax that appeared in 1836. Titled *Awful Disclosure of Maria Monk,* it supposedly contained the personal revelations of a nun who had escaped from a Montreal convent, and who told of 'criminal intercourse' between nuns and priests and the baptism and immediate strangulation of babies born of those unions. The books was actually written by a delinquent girl who had never even been inside a convent, but it was so popular among anti-Catholic forces that it went through 20 printings and sold 300,000 copies in the 25 years after it appeared.

The Irish attitude toward the American political process was different, too, and their organized and aggressive approach to politics and growing strength at the polls also worried many American nativists — who wanted to preserve a homogen-

MIKE WALSH.

The People's Champion
*And Leader of the Young or progressive Democracy, Nominated by the Democratic Party in Tammany
Hall and Elected to the New York Legislature in Nov. 1846.*

eous, Protestant, Anglo-Saxon United States. The Naturalization Act of 1802 had rescinded the severe 1798 laws that raised the residency requirement for citizenship from five to fourteen years, and by the 1830s most states had eliminated all property and taxpayer qualifications for voting; New York did so in 1826. By the mid-1830s state legislatures had also struck down any anti-Catholic laws on their books. With their full voting rights thus guaranteed, Irish-Americans began to make their presence felt on Election Day.

The agitation for reform that was sweeping Ireland, beginning in the 1820s, had helped prepare the Irish in America to seize this opportunity. In the old country, led by Catholic barrister Daniel O'Connell, the 'uncrowned king of Ireland', the people learned to use their hard-earned right to vote to pressure the British government for change. In 1823 O'Connell founded the Catholic Association and enlisted a large membership that staged mass demonstrations for him and recruited new supporters, aided by contributions from many chapters of the Friends of Ireland, which was begun in New York City in 1828 to further the cause of Catholic emancipation. After O'Connell won election to the House of Commons he was at first refused entry because he objected to the demeaning loyalty oath required of Catholic M.P.s, but his electoral victory prompted the passage of the Catholic Relief Bill in 1829; he later worked unsuccessfully for repeal of the Act of Union. Casting a vote for O'Connell often required real courage and commitment for an Irish farmer, because ballots were not secret and many landlords summarily evicted tenants who did not vote for the Ascendancy candidate. By working toward emancipation, however, Irish Catholics learned how to manipulate the constitutional system to their advantage — and discovered that they could do so successfully. When they arrived in America they carried their strong and growing sense of national identity and their hard-won political savvy with them.

The key to Irish political strength in New York City was their domination of the Democratic Party through the Tammany Hall organization. They had always felt at home in the egalitarian party of Thomas Jefferson and Andrew Jackson, whom they helped re-elect to a second term as President in 1832. Local party leaders arranged for new arrivals to be quickly naturalized and registered as voters, and won support by dispensing patronage jobs in the local police and fire departments and generally looking after their constituents when they were burned out, arrested or lost a job. In return, the Irish could generally be counted on to vote straight a Democratic ticket, and gangs of Irish 'bhoys' often protected Democratic candidates and harrassed their opponents.

Mike Walsh's career is typical of the rapid Irish rise to prominence in New York City politics. Born in 1815, he came to the States with his parents as a child and grew up as the Irish were first beginning to flex their new political muscle. A natural orator and crowd-pleaser, Walsh won a large popular following by speaking out against the exploitation of Irish laborers, and was an early advocate of worker solidarity and labor unionism. He bent the Tammany system to his own purposes by exposing the power tactics of its nomating committees, eventually getting himself nominated and elected to the New York State Assembly and later to Congress, where he served until his death in 1859. By opening the doors of Tammany to Irish participation, Walsh set an important precedent for other aspiring politicians in the Irish-American community to follow.

Nativist adversaries of the Irish, however, resented and feared this eruption of 'Irish power' at the polls, and accused them of voting 'early — and often' for the Democratic slate. It was just one more reason to hate the foreigners, and there were soon signs that nativist ethnic and religious prejudices were beginning to heat up. Many earlier Protestant Irish immigrants from Ulster began calling themselves 'Scotch-Irish', to distinguish themselves from the mass of predominantly Catholic newcomers. 'No Irish need apply' became a common addendum to ads for household help and other workers. These are typical:

WANTED. A Cook or a Chambermaid. They must be American, Scotch, Swiss, or Africans — no Irish.
New York Evening Post, *Sept. 4, 1830*

WANTED. A woman well qualified to take charge of the cooking and washing of a family — any one but a Catholic who can come

CHAPTER THREE

LEFT *Born in Ireland and brought to America as a child in 1815, Mike Walsh became a vocal political spokesman for impoverished Irish immigrants. He was elected to the New York State Legislature in 1846 and to Congress in 1850, where he served until his death in 1859.*

New-York

FICE, 16 BROAD-STREET.

FRIDAY EVENING, JANUARY 7, 18

ACKET SHIPS.

NDON LINE OF PACKETS.

Packets is now composed of the following Ships, from London and New-York in regular succes- ondon on the 10th and Portsmouth on the 15th of d New-York on the 16th, viz.:
ON, E. E. Morgan, master—
ew-York on 16th January, May, and September.
ondon on 10th March, July, and November.
ortsmouth on 15th March, July, and November.
REIGN, H. L. Champlin, master—
ew-York on 16th February, June, and October.
ondon on 10th April, August, and December.
ortsmouth on 15th April, August, and December.
RIA, Geo. Moore, master—
ew-York on 16th March, July, and November.
ondon on 10th May, September, and January.
ortsmouth on 15th May, September, and January.
DENT, C. H. Champlin, master—
ew-York on 16th April, August, and December.
ondon on 10th February, June, and October.
ortsmouth on 15th February, June, and October.
entioned Ships are all of the first class, coppered tened, and are fitted and furnished in the most elegant manner, and will be profusely supplied , and Stores, and Wines, &c. of the best descrip- Commanders (who are well known) will exert n all occasions to facilitate the wishes of Shippers by these Packets, and to oblige and accommo- s.
r passage, apply to either of the Commanders of e Agents in London, Messrs. GEO. WILDES & leman street; or to
OHN GRISWOLD, Agent at New-York,
69 South street, corner of Pine street.
hips of the above Line will continue to touch at ch way, to land and receive passengers. Steam- e to the Continent, and to differen parts of Eng- d18

LINE OF LONDON PACKETS.

RIA, J. S. Delano, master, to sail 1st February.
AL, F. H. Hebard, master, to sail 1st March.
HIAN, D. Chadwick, master, to sail 1st April.
ON, H. Huttleston, master, to sail 16th April.
O, Wm. S. Sebor, master, to sail 1st May.
to offer to the public greater facilities in the in- en New-York and London, the subscribers have above Ships as a Line of Packets, to sail from the 1st, and London on the 25th of each month in y are ships of the first class—about 400 tons bur astened and coppered—commanded by men ex- e trade—and no expense will be spared in ma- mmodations convenient and comfortable for pas , Bedding, Wines, and Stores, of the first quality,
or Passage, apply to the masters on board, or to FISH, GRINNELL & CO. 134 Front street.
hips of the above Line are intended to touch at ch way, for the purpose of landing and receiving Steamboats run constantly from that place to the to different parts of England. j4

LIVERPOOL PACKETS.

bers have established the following ships as a s between this port and Liverpool—to leave this , and Liverpool on the 24th of each month in the
Ira Bursley, master, to sail 8th January.
E CANNING, Frs. Allyn, master, to sail 8th Feb
EON, John P. Smith, master, to sail 8th March.
RICHARDS, H. Holdrege, master, to sail 8th April
are about 500 tons each, built of the best materi- stened and coppered, commanded by men experi- rade, and no expense will be spared in making odations convenient and comfortable for passen- Bedding, Wines, and Stores, of the first quality, . For freight or passage, apply to the captains on
FISH, GRINNELL & CO. 134 Front-street.

PACKETS FOR HAVRE.

ndermentioned ships will sail—
HAM, Capt. Depeyster, will sail from New-York anuary—and Havre 1st March.
RD BONNAFFE, Capt. Hathaway, will sail from rk on 20th January—and Havre 10th March.
LEMAGNE, Capt. H. Robinson, will sail from rk on 1st February—and Havre 20th March.
E., Capt. Keene, will sail from New-York on 10th y—and Havre 1st April.
LES CARROLL, Capt. J. Clark, will sail from rk on 20th February—and Havre 10th April.
RD QUESNEL, Capt. E. Hawkins, will sail from rk on 1st March—and Havre 20th April.
I IV, Capt. J. B. Pell, will sail from New-York March—and Havre 1st May.
Capt. Jas. Funk, will sail from New-York on 20th and Havre 10th May.
Y, Capt. W. W. Pell, will sail from New-York on —and Havre 20th May.

SCHOOLS.

SCHOOL No. 184 FULTON STREET.

MISS ORAM would inform her friends and the public, that her School for Young Ladies, is now reorganized and ready for the reception of pupils. From her long experience and willingness to devote herself to the instruction of children, she dares promise that every means will be used, in the school under her care, to promote their improvement. Mr. Weisse, a gentleman from Paris, will teach French. He wll give instruction according to Mr. Manesca's system, which enables children to speak and write French from their first lesson (according to the knowledge given of it): indeed they cannot progress, only as they are able to understand, pronounce and write their own lessons. This method upon investigation will speak for itself, and those interested in education, have only to become acquainted with it, to see its superiority over that, which condemns children to study an abstract grammar of a foreign language, when they are yet unable to comprehend their own. Mr. George Geib will instruct in Music. The tuition of every department of the school will be given according to the principles of Analysis and Association. n30 tf

SCHOOL FOR BOYS.

MR. RICHARD P. JENKS will open his PREPARATORY SCHOOL FOR BOYS on Monday, the first of November next, in one of the basement rooms of the Church, at the corner of Prince and Mercer-streets.

The Studies to be pursued are, Reading, Spelling, Writing, Grammar, Mental Arithmetic, Written Arithmetic (the simple rules) by dictation, and French.

No pupil will be admitted over *ten* years of age.

Terms, $10 per quarter, (*in advance*) including every charge except that of Books and Stationary.

Applications for entrance, or for a circular describing more fully the plan and objects of the School, may be made at No. 95 Spring-street, where Mr. J. will be happy to answer any inquiries.

References.—The Faculty of Harvard University; Rev. Dr. Spring; Rev. George Upfold; Dr. Jeremiah Van Rensselaer; David B. Ogden, Esq.; R. M. Blatchford, Esq.; J. Green Pearson, Esq. of New-York: and Theodore Eames, Esq. Brooklyn, (L. I.) N5

FRENCH LANGUAGE.

Taught according to the methods of Horne Tooke, Court de Gebelin Roubaud and others.

M. STANISLAS, lately editor of the *Courrier des Etats Unis*, proposes to give instruction in the French language, according to the methods above referred to. His course will be, to reduce each compound word to its simplest elements; to distinguish the principal *primitives*, that is to say, the roots expressing the principal ideas, from the *prepositives* and *terminatives*, or those roots which enter into the composition of different families of words, and only express secondary ideas. He will seek to establish the primitive value of both; and the different acceptations in which each may be taken or used, according to the immutable laws of the association of ideas: he will arrange words according to their *families*, and in the order of their descent.

According to other methods, each separate word appears to be selected at hazard; and the knowledge of it is of no avail towards acquiring the knowledge of others; hence language appears to be a mere *chaos* of heterogeneous elements. By this method, on the contrary, there is a reason for every word, in its intimate and natural connexion with the thing signified: it becomes a living animated picture of it: the alarming number of twenty-seven thousand words in the French language, is reduced to a few families: the acquaintance with a single member of this family, insures an acquaintance with all the others, and recalls them to the mind, by associating them with each other; the memory is relieved from an oppressive weight; light extends through all parts of the language; the imagination is flattered; the understanding satisfied, and reason proceeds with a sure and rapid step.

Classes for gentlemen in the evening, and for young ladies in the afternoon, will shortly commence. Those who wish to join are requested to apply immediately.

Any person who would test the merits of the above method, is invited to take fifteen lessons; and, if he is not convinced that it is a most certain and short way of teaching and learning the French, he may withdraw without any expense.

For terms, apply at the subscriber's, where a sketch of the method will be found.

s21 STANISLAS, Reed-street, No. 19.

FRENCH SCHOOL.

M. & MADAME BERTEAU, propose opening at their House, No. 66 *Lispenard-street*, on the first of next month, a Day School for Boys under eight, and girls under ten, years of age. Instruction in Reading, Writing, Geography, Arithmetic, and the other elementary branches will be given exclusively through the French, and every exertion will be made to enable the Pupils that may be placed under their care, to acquire the proper pronunciation of this most important language, and to speak it with ease and fluency. The young ladies will be taught Needlework, &c.

The School will be open every day except Saturday, from 9 till 2 o'clock. Terms, $10 per quarter.

School in session from the 10th of September to the 31st of July. Quarters commence on the 10th of September, 1st of December, 20th of February, and the 10th of May; but pupils are received at any intermediate period, the proportion of the quarter only being charged.

M. and Madame Berteau refer to the following certificate from the Hon. G. C. Verplanck, and other literary gentlemen.—

"Convinced that a foreign language can only be learned, so as to be used with satisfaction and pleasure, in early youth, when the organs are flexible, we earnestly recommend to the attention of parents the above notice of M. and Madame Berteau, in whose qualifications we have full confidence. Their proposition affords an opportunity of accomplishing a most important object at little expense, and at a time of life when it is difficult to find equally advantageous occupation for children.

November 23d, 1830.

G. C. VERPLANCK, CHARLES G. TROUP,
n29tf W. B. LAWRENCE, CHARLES KING.

DANCING ACADEMY FOR LADIES AND CHILDREN.

M

SCHOOLS.

MRS. THOMAS MORRIS'
BOARDING & DAY SCHOOL FOR YOUNG LADIES—
At Greenwich,

IS NOW OPEN for the reception of Pupils. Mrs. Morris has engaged the assistance of competent masters in every branch of education. n5 2m

PRIVATE LITERARY INSTITUTE,
No. 381 BROADWAY.

THE WINTER CLASSES of the *French and Spanish Languages* for Gentlemen, under the tuition of Mr. O. DE A. SANTANGELO, will commence on the first Monday of January next—to be continued every evening, from 6 to 10 o'clock.

Mr. S. will also commence his Spanish and Italian Courses at the Columbia College on the second Tuesday of January, in the afternoon. Private Lessons given as usual. The English Language taught to foreigners on the most successful plan.

Gentlemen desirous of practising during the day, or even of learning *grammatically* the above foreign languages, may be comfortably accommodated, on very moderate terms, as Boarders in the Institute.

The cares of Mad. Santangelo being now limited to the scientific and moral education of young ladies as *day scholars*, her exertions, in connexion with those of other teachers of the highest merit, will be redoubled for their instruction (five hours every morning) in Writing, English Grammar, Arithmetic, Geography, (for which splendid maps have been procured) History, Mythology, Embroidery, Manners, &c., as well as in the French, Spanish, and Italian Languages, and in Singing, and Music on the Piano, or Guitar, &c. Music will be taught after MERCADANTE's MUSICAL GRAMMAR, hitherto unknown in the United States, and by which the *science* of Music may be easily and *thoroughly* learned in a few months. The plan of this instruction, and the importance of its effects, are explained in a card, which may be had at the Institute. Terms for Music $20 per quarter, three lessons a week *of two hours each*, given partly in class, partly individually, with the privilege of studying the Italian language without charge. For all other branches of the English or Foreign Education, terms as hitherto. d29 4w

DANCING SCHOOL,
280 Broadway and 169 Mott st., three doors above Broome st.

TWELFTH CLASS—E. H. CONWAY respectfully informs the public, that his Twelfth Class for gentlemen will commence on Tuesday the 4th, at 169 Mott street, at 7 oclock in the evening. His Thirteenth Class for gentlemen will commence at 280 Broadway, on Wednesday evening at 7 o'clock. His first class for ladies and pupils under the age of fourteen, will commence their second quarter on Tuesday the 4th, at 3 o'clock. Persons who are desirous of joining either of these classes, will have the goodness to leave their names on or before the above dates. Three gentlemen will be admitted in a private class, if they apply immediately.

Days of Tuition at 169 Mott-street—Tuesdays and Saturdays, from 3 to 5 for ladies and pupils under the age of fourteen;—Tuesday and Thursday evenings from 7 to 9 for gentlemen.

At 280 Broadway—Wednesday and Friday from 3 to 5 for ladies and pupils under the age of fourteen; Wednesday and Friday evenings from 7 to 9 for gentlemen.

A public Cotilion Party on each Monday evening during the season. d30

BOYS' CLOTHING EMPORIUM,
No. 381 Broadway, corner of White street.

THE only Extensive Establishment in New York, devoted exclusively to BOYS' CLOTHES, where an extensive assortment, made up in the best style, of various patterns, to suit Boys of all ages and the different tastes of parents, is kept constantly on hand for sale.

MOURNING DRESSES for Boys of any age furnished at the shortest notice, without the delay ordinarily attendant on occasions of family afflictions, by

JAS. A. CAMPFIELD, Draper and Tailor.

NB. Gentlemen's Clothing made to order at the shortest notice. [F2] d24

B. KNORINE,
No. 148 Church street,

ICE CREAM MAKER, from the celebrated Establishment of TORTONI, in Paris, has the honor to inform the public that he will supply Families and Societies, in all seasons and in the best style, with all sorts of Ice Cream, Punch a la Romaine, Punch Glace, &c. at the shortest notice.

He also receives *Orders for DINNERS*, which will be punctually attended to, and sent to any part of the city.

NB.—SYRUPS of every description to be had.

☞ Mr. K. has just received from Paris a number of very beautiful Forms for his Ices. He has permission to refer to persons of the first respectability. d20

PIANO FORTE WAREHOUSE.

R. & W. NUNNS respectfully inform their friends and the public that they have always on hand an assortment of Cabinet, Harmonic, and Square Piano Fortes, from their Manufactory, at their Warehouse, No. 127 Broadway, two doors north of the City Hotel.

The extensive sale which the instruments of their manufacture have had throughout the United States for seven years, has made them so well known as to preclude the necessity of their saying any thing with regard to the quality of the instruments bearing their name. They can only add, that the result of many years experience in this branch of manufacture, added to the extended scale they are prepared to carry it on, will enable them to afford advantages to purchasers equal to any other house in the Union.

Orders from the country punctually attended to, and old Piano Fortes taken in exchange. n27

ORNAMENTAL HAIR MANUFACTORY,
No. 204 Broadway.

GILBERT, MANUEL and GODQUIN, Hair Dressers thankful for past favors, respectfully inform the Ladies and Gentlemen of New York, that they have received by the last arrivals, from their house in Paris, a large assortment of Unmanufactured Hair, of the best quality, and at very low rates; which has enabled them to reduce the price of their Ornamental Hair such as Frissets, Puffs, Ringlets, Braids, &c.

Country dealers are respectfully invited to visit their long

NOTICE

OCEAN INSURANCE

THE President and Directors of the pany have this day declared a regular D on their Capital Stock for the last six after Monday next, the 10th instant.
By order of the Board,
J3 2w JAS. S. SCHERME

NEPTUNE INSURANC

A DIVIDEND of Six per cent. on th last six months has been declared this d at the Office of the Company, No. 25, M
By order. A. B. N
J3 2w

FARMERS' FIRE INSURA COMPANY—No. 34

THE Board of Directors of this Com clared a Dividend of *three and a half* stock, payable at their Office on and aft ary next. The Transfer Book will be c
December 16, 1830. JOH
d17 1m

FRANKLIN FIRE INSUR

THE Annual Election for Sixteen Di will be held at the Office, No. 1, on Monday, the 10th day of January n open from 12 to 2 o'clock, and the Tra the 1st prox. until after the election. B
d22tJ10 J. WORTHI

GLOBE INSURANCE

THE President and Directors give n Three and one half per cent. on the Ca pany for the last six months, will be paid their Office, No. 27 Wall-street, on a December next. The Transfer Books 21st instant. RICHARD
November 10th, 1830.

UNITED STATES FIRE COMPANY.

THE Board of Directors have this d of Three and a half per Cent. payable their representatives on or after the 1st fer Books will be closed on the 29th inst.
ANDREW
New York, 16th November, 1830.

NEPTUNE INSURANCE

AN ELECTION for Directors of Company of the City of New-York will be held at the Office of the Comp Exchange, on Monday, the 10th day of J be open from 12 to 1 o'clock, P. M. By
d31 1w A. B. N

EAGLE FIRE COMPANY O

THE ANNUAL ELECTION for D ny will be held at the Office on Tu ry. The poll will open at 12, and close
d31 t11J THOMAS G

THE President and Directors have th dend of three and one half per cent. for th able at their office, No. 53 Wall-street, o
J4 1m NATHL.

HOWARD INSURANC

A DIVIDEND of Four per cent. upo the last six months, was this day decla rectors, payable on and after the 10th ins
LEWIS P
January 3d, 1831.

UNION INSURANCE

THE ANNUAL ELECTION for year, will be held at the Office of the chants' Exchange, on Monday, the 10th be open from half past one, to half past t
New-York, 3d January, 1831.
J3 t10 WM. J. VAN WA

COPARTNERS

EDWARD A. GRAVES, and N have this day associated with them J late of the firm of Meert & Graves. Th tinued as heretofore, under the firm Sons.

EAGLE FIRE COMPANY

THE Board of Directors have this of four per cent. upon the Capi months, payable on or after the 15th ins
New-York, 4th January, 1831.
j5 3w THOMAS

MANHATTAN CO

THE MANHATTAN COMPANY Dividend of Three and a half per cen the Stockholders on or after the 10th in
J6 1w ROBERT W

NOTICE.

THE Copartnership heretofore exi W. W. & E. Thompson, is this day di of the same will be settled by either of t
W.
ED
1st mo. 1st, 1831.

NOTICE.

THE subscribers have this day ente under the firm of Francis, Thompson tion of Commission Business.
J
W
January 1st, 1831.

NOTICE.

well recommended, may call at 57 John Street.

Journal of Commerce, *July 8, 1830*

Smoldering ethnic and religious prejudices finally ignited, sparked by the unprecedented and tension-ridden growth of the cities and competition for jobs. Open warfare erupted, and major cities along the Eastern seaboard witnessed more than 35 major riots over the next 20 years. In 1831 St. Mary's Church in New York City was set afire, and demonstrations followed. In 1834, rioters in Charlestown, Massachusetts, ransacked and burned an Ursuline convent that stood next to historic Bunker Hill; seven of the eight men tried in the incident were acquitted and the eighth was later pardoned when local Catholics, as a conciliatory gesture, asked for clemency. Three years later, in 1837, Boston was the scene of the Bond Street riot. The worst unrest, however, developed in Philadelphia in 1844, after a long history of election disputes, fights between volunteer fire companies and other conflicts. When Bishop Francis Kenrick, a native of Dublin, convinced the school board to exempt Catholic children from religious instruction and to let them read the Douay version of the Bible in public school, Protestants staged an angry meeting and fighting eruped. After a man carrying an American flag was killed, nativist mobs raged through Irish Kensington, rioting and burning. More fighting broke out in July when word spread that the pastor of St. Philip Neri had stored guns in the church basement. This time the state militia were called in to protect Catholic churches, but a battle broke out between the militia and the nativists and went on for days. By the time calm returned to the city, over 50 people were dead and over 100 wounded; more than 200 families had been burned out and three churches had been destroyed. New York's Catholic churches escaped only because fighting Bishop John Hughes, from County Tyrone, surrounded them with armed guards and threatened to torch the city and turn it into a 'second Moscow' if one parish church was desecrated.

Many Americans were appalled by this lawless violence, which reminded them of the infamous horrors of the French Revolution. But the nativist movement did not expire until after a final campaign by the Know-Nothing Party in the 1850s. By then, however, the Irish on both sides of the Atlantic were engulfed by a new crisis of unprecedented proportions that would transform the American Irish community — and the American nation itself — forever.

CHAPTER THREE

LEFT *"No Irish need apply." The sad fact of discrimination against the Irish is shown in this newspaper of 1831. The first advertisement under "Wants" states "Wanted a cook — She must not be an Irish woman . . . "*

ABOVE *Major-general Philip Sheridan and his generals in front*
of Sheridan's tent in 1864. Sheridan is third from left.

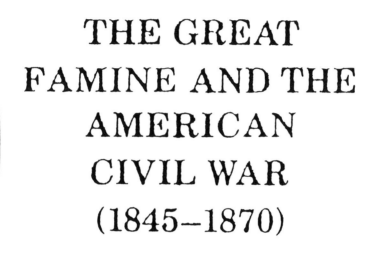

THE GREAT FAMINE AND THE AMERICAN CIVIL WAR (1845–1870)

CHAPTER FOUR

fter Sir Walter Raleigh carried the potato from America to Ireland it spread rapidly throughout most of the island, and by the 1800s it was all that kept the majority of peasants alive on their tiny farms. An acre of potatoes could feed a large family; an acre of wheat could not.

So when an unknown fungus suddenly struck and destroyed the crop in the summer of 1845, people were terrified. "This country . . . is greatly alarmed on account of a disease in the Potatoe Crop," admitted a farmer's wife, "we are feeling the effect of it but God knows not how it will end." Everyone waited anxiously for the next harvest. By August 1846, however, it was obvious that the plants were almost completely wiped out. The blight subsided the following year, but the discouraged farmers had planted so few potatoes that they dug up only one-tenth the number they had grown in 1844; subsequent harvests were cut to less than half the 1844 level before the disease finally subsided in 1855.

The Potato Famine was the most important event in modern Irish — and Irish-American — history. It destroyed not only the potato crop but many small farms and farmers and much of traditional Irish culture along with them, and turned an entire generation into refugees; only one of every three Irishmen born around 1831 died at home in Ireland. More than one person in four either perished of starvation or disease or emigrated; out of a population of nine million, over two million fled, and more than a million did not survive long enough to escape. Perhaps half a million people were evicted and left to beg for their food, often because they had consumed their grain or livestock instead of selling iot to pay their rent. Weakened by malnutrition, thousands succumbed to typhus, cholera, scurvy, relapsing fever and dysentery.

Although over three million were being fed daily by 1847, British famine relief generally was grudging and insufficient. It was designed primarily to keep the Irish from becoming economically 'dependent'. The British government sponsored public works projects and parcelled out Indian corn imported from America, but laissez-faire advocates refused to control food speculators and continued to export Irish cattle and grain while the population starved and food prices soared. Some Protestant agencies also distributed free food to the poor, but Catholics accused many of doing so only after the recipients promised to abandon 'popery'. The converts were later disdainfully labelled 'soupers' after the soup kitchens that fed them. Irish and British Quakers were particularly active in famine relief, and the Irish in America sent millions of dollars in cash and foodstuffs to help their stricken friends and relatives.

Too often, however, such help did not arrive in time. One Quaker relief worker described the country after the 'starving winter' of 1846–47: "The town of Westport was itself a strange and fearful sight . . . its streets crowded with gaunt wanderers, saunting to and fro with hopeless air and hunger-struck look; a mob of starved, almost naked, women around the poorhouse, clamoring for soup tickets." After visiting a rural district he reported that, "Out of a population of 240 I found thirteen already dead from want. The survivors were like walking skeletons — the men gaunt and haggard, stamped with the livid mark of hunger — the children crying with pain — the women in some of the cabins too weak to stand."

Families were torn apart; people wandered the countryside scavenging for stray turnips and ate grass, seaweed, shellfish and dead animals. Those that died were often buried unceremoniously in mass graves when the supply of coffins ran out.

There was even a shortage of ships to carry away the desperate refugees who could scrape together money for their passage. Many fled in a panic, without enough food or clothing for the journey, crowding aboard the notorious 'coffin ships' for a dangerous midwinter voyage rather than waiting for better weather. So many were already ill and weak from hunger that close to a third of those sailing to Canada died before or shortly after landing; among passengers who could afford the more expensive American ships the death rate was one in ten. Thousands who were too sick to land at U.S. ports were diverted by quarantine ships to the Canadian quarantine station at Grosse Ile, Quebec; in 1847 alone at least 30,000 died at sea or in quarantine after arrival, including 5,424 who perished at the Canadian hospital and several doctors who treated them for typhus and other diseases. Another quarantine station on Staten Island, at the entrance to New York harbor, was attacked by island residents in 1854 as a 'pestilence breeder'.

During the height of the Famine, as many as 30 or 40 ships a day landed in New York. Frauds and outright attacks on newcomers at the docks multiplied until the state was forced to pass laws regulating runners and boardinghouse keepers. Arrival remained a harrowing experience until the new Castle Garden reception center was

CHAPTER FOUR

LEFT *The predominantly Irish servants of the Stevens family gather for a group portrait in 1895. Domestic service was a major source of employment for first-generation Irish-American women.*

opened in 1856, where runners were excluded and immigrants could get their money changed at the legal rate, check listings of reputable boarding-houses, and find inexpensive food and free rest-rooms and hot water.

The Irish who left during these Famine years were not the truly destitute, but they were still poorer than most of the earlier emigrants, and there were more women and family groups, more children and elderly. Many were also Irish speakers and traditionalists who were slower to adapt to new ways, and a large number had no skills other than growing potatoes.

In 1846, three-quarters of those sailing to New York were either laborers or servants. Nine out of ten were probably Catholic. As a group, the Famine immigrants found it harder to adjust to life in America than those who had come before them.

There were some notable exceptions, of course. Patrick Kennedy, the great-grandfather of the President, left County Wexford after selling everything he owned to buy a one-way ticket to Boston in 1849. Once arrived, he laid the founda-tion for his family's resounding commercial and political successes.

The majority of Famine immigrants, however, were forced to take jobs as domestics or day-laborers and found it hard to advance beyond the lowest rungs of the socio-economic ladder. "It is not so very easy to get Muney heer as we all [thought] when [we] were to home," one new-comer wrote to her friends in Cork; "You have to work hard to make one pound." Life in Ireland had not prepared them for large-scale American farming, and most settled in the commercial and industrial centers of the Northeast and Midwest: in New York, Philadelphia, Boston and Balti-more; in manufacturing towns like Troy, Lowell and Poughkeepsie; in Detroit, Milwaukee and South Bend. Even those who might have wanted to strike out beyond the cities where they landed often could not muster the fortitude or funds to do so. One woman complained after her family had arrived in New York that, "We were determined . . . to proceed to some of the Western States but from sickness and disappointments we were obliged to remain in this City, which have nearly ex-hausted our little Capitol, [since] employment is impossible to be found . . ." Urban American so-ciety was by now more stratified and offered the immigrants fewer opportunities to move up. In Philadelphia, for example, one percent of the 1860 population owned 50 percent of the city's real estate and personal property, while the lower 80 percent of the residents were left with 3 percent of it to divide among themselves. In addition, suc-ceeding in America usually took more single-

CHAPTER FOUR

RIGHT *Boston in the 1850s was a strongly Irish, strongly Catholic seaport city.*

BELOW RIGHT *These bearded Irish clamdiggers and their matronly companion were photographed on a wharf in Boston in 1882.*

FAR RIGHT *The notorious Five Points section, an Irish neighborhood of New York City, in 1859. New immigrants were often directed here by unscrupulous "runners" and then fleeced of their money. Note the "House of Industry" (a euphemism for workhouse) at upper left, and the women smoking pipes.*

minded determination, business sense, familiarity with the culture and sheer good luck than most of these first-generation immigrants could muster. As a result, during the 1850s a third of New York City's voters were Irish-born, but four out of five of the city's servants and waiters were Irish, as were one out of every four policemen.

Many willing hands inevitably meant lower wages, and the Famine Irish squeezed into neighborhoods already overflowing with their fellow countrymen, taking whatever housing their dollar-a-day earnings would buy. While greedy middlemen profited from the shortage of decent living space, Irish families crowded into converted factories, cramped garrets or damp, unhealthy, windowless cellars. One official Health Department report told about a New York City family of three — parents and their 12-year-old daughter — who shared a low-ceilinged room 5½ by 9 feet where the father also worked making shoes! Forced to live under such conditions, up to 80 percent of Irish babies in New York City died soon after birth, and many families lost a father by his late 30s or early 40s in a factory or construction accident and lost a mother, brothers or sisters to bronchitis, consumption or cancer.

If their Yankee neighbors had been dismayed at the 'Irishtowns' they saw springing up around them in the 1830s and 1840s, they were even more disturbed at this new and massive influx of immigrants. The population of New York City doubled between 1840 and 1855, and by 1860 it had more Irish-born residents than any other city in the world, including Dublin — over a quarter of its 805,651 inhabitants. Across the river in Brooklyn, where Irish neighborhoods grew up near the waterfront facing Manhattan, more than one out of every five residents was born abroad.

The Five Points section of lower Manhattan became a teeming slum that other New Yorkers found fascinating but disturbing. Irish shantytowns appeared along the northern borders of Central Park, and when the Irish livestock that had immigrated along with their owners began to multiply, neighbors called police to insist that they break up the 'piggeries'. More doors slammed shut, and more 'No Irish Need Apply' signs appeared on shops and businesses. Anti-Irish jokes made the rounds, poking fun at the newcomers' unfamiliarity with urban American ways, like the one about the Irish cook who accidentally dropped some candles in a pail of water and put them in the oven to dry, or the Irish maid who was sent to the store for a 'bed comforter' by her mistress and returned with one of the clerks.

The Irish did not give up. Instead, they fought back their homesickness and gathered their courage. Bound together by their hardships, they were also united by a growing spirit of nationalism that was fed by the new wave of immigrants who, particularly after the horrors of the Famine years, blamed England for their forced 'exile' in an increasingly inhospitable new land. Back in Ireland, many landlords resented the Poor Law of 1838, which taxed them to support their indigent leaseholders, and had welcomed the chance to clear their lands of poor tenant farmers. One Limerick landlord acknowledged that, "I could not have got rid of them by any means, if it had not been for the failure of the potato crop". This callous attitude was shared by some key figures in the British government, particularly after the Whig Lord John Russell replaced Tory Robert Peel as Prime Minister. Charles Trevelyan, who was head of the Treasury and directed the Whigs' famine relief programs, believed that the blight was sent by God to punish the wicked Irish, and a noted Whig economist named Nassau Senior considered the Famine beneficial to the extent that it solved the problem of overpopulation in Ireland.

Irish-Americans were furious when they heard about such sentiments, and rallied behind a new nationalist movement called Young Ireland, which had split with Daniel O'Connell's National Repeal Association after he condemned the use of force in the struggle to free Ireland. Its founders were Thomas Davis, John Blake Dillon and Charles Gavan Duffy, law students at the King's Inn in Dublin, and their newspaper, *The Nation,* which they started in 1842, became the voice of Irish cultural identity in America as well as in Ireland. That same year, Irish-Americans met nationally for the first time. On Washington's Birthday in Philadelphia, delegates from 26 different cities and towns came together to affirm their unity and to demand that England repeal the 1800 Act of Union, which had abolished the

CHAPTER FOUR

Independent Irish Parliament and made the two countries one.

Irish-Americans consumed the nationalist essays and poetry they found in *The Nation* and eagerly collected arms and money for the Young Irelanders' planned insurrection. The masses of Irish were too hard-hit by the Famine, however, to stage a successful revolution, and the largely middle-class Young Ireland movement had little support among the peasants and those who still looked to O'Connell for leadership. The revolt began and ended in a brief skirmish in a cabbage field with the Royal Irish Constabulary on July 29, 1848. Many of the 'Men of '48' fled to America, where they were honored as heroes and continued to write and work for Irish freedom.

Among the rebellion's leaders were William Smith O'Brien, Terence Bellew McManus, John Mitchel, Thomas Francis Meagher and Thomas D'Arcy McGee. After being banished to Tasmania with O'Brien, Mitchel, Meagher and McManus escaped to America. Although Mitchel supported the Confederacy and was pro-slavery, Meagher later served as an acclaimed Union officer during the Civil War, and McGee founded a new version of *The Nation* and *The American Celt* before moving to Canada, where he started another paper called *The New Era*. He was active in provincial politics and gained election to the first Dominion parliament in 1867, but was assassinated the following year by an Irish nationalist for condemning the Fenian raids into Canada.

The Fenian Brotherhood was a secret, nationalist revolutionary organization committed to violent struggle to achieve Irish independence. Named after the Fianna, a legendary band of Gaelic warriors, it was founded in New York in 1858 by two Young Irelanders, James Stephens and John O'Mahony, and a third Irishman, Michael Doheny. The European arm of the movement was christened the Irish Republican Brotherhood. By 1860, when O'Mahony started a nationalist newspaper to serve as the movement's mouthpiece, there were Fenian groups in most of the nation's Irish-American communities. The Church officially condemned them for their secrecy and involvement with 'anarchy and bloodshed'. Membership and contributions grew slowly. But by 1865 the seven-year-old Fenian Brotherhood was 50,000 members strong and had hundreds of thousands more supporters, making it the most formidable ethnic organization in Irish America. After the Civil War ended, some newly discharged Irish soldiers traveled to Ireland to train potential rebels. Other veteran soldiers

made up much of the Fenian 'army' that invaded Canada in 1866 and again in 1870. Their aims: to take the country hostage and exchange it later for a free Ireland; to begin a revolution there and in Ireland; to strike a blow at the British Empire.

While their European counterparts organized secret revolutionary cells, the American Fenians were true to the traditions of their adopted homeland. They held a convention in Philadelphia in 1865 and also drafted a constitution outlining a government based on a president and congress. They flew the harp-and-sunburst flag over their national capitol in a mansion on New York's Union Square, raised hundreds of thousands of dollars through bond sales to support their 'government in exile' and its activities, and even chose a Secretary of War, General Thomas W. Sweeny, who had distinguished himself in the Mexican War and the Civil War.

A split had developed in the organization in 1865 after several members of its Irish arm were arrested. One American Fenian faction insisted on preparing for an eventual uprising in Ireland, and several hundred Irish-American officers did help lead an unsuccessful IRB insurrection there in 1867. A second faction, however, immediately set about collecting funds, recruiting soldiers and holding rallies — one of which, in March 1866, drew over 100,000 Irish to the picnic grounds in New York's Yorkville section. Then they picked the first week of June 1866 for their invasion.

Militia companies were summoned from as far away as Louisiana and Iowa, and ordered to gather at predetermined locations to prepare for the attack. There were to be three separate invasion forces. One was to assembly along the Vermont border, one in Chicago and the main body in Buffalo, New York. Canadian spies knew all about the invasion plans, however, and the English had their own informer. Meanwhile, the U.S. government, which had until now allowed the Fenians to operate freely, had been monitoring arms shipments to the border, but was unwilling to stop them because it did not want to provoke Irish-American voters. Besides, the British had helped the Confederacy and had not yet made amends.

The main Fenian invasionary force was made up largely of Civil War veterans and was led by John O'Neill, a Civil War captain, who took 800 men of the 'Irish Republican Army' across the Niagara River on May 31 and captured the town of Fort Erie. Jubilantly, his troops hoisted their flag over the vanquished British settlement. He soon learned that a couple of British units were

approaching, however, and hurried to meet them, defeating a larger Canadian force on June 2 at the Battle of Limestone Ridge. The invasion ended when the U.S. gunboat *Michigan* prevented any more men or supplies from reaching O'Neill's and his troops, and he and his followers were arrested on June 3 as they retreated across the river to Buffalo. All told, eight Fenians had been killed and twenty wounded, while the Canadians counted twelve dead and forty wounded. The Vermont Fenian force also managed to make its way into Canada, but was driven back after capturing a British flag.

In 1870, a second attempt to invade Canada was set for May 24, Queen Victoria's birthday. O'Neill led an attack by 200 men at Franklin, Vermont, a day late, but the Canadians were ready. The troops exchanged gunfire, and the Fenians were driven back. O'Neill was arrested by the U.S. marshall while riding to get reinforcements and was charged with violating the neutrality laws. A second force that had assembled at Malone, New York, was hardly across the border before they were forced back again.

After this second defeat, Fenian volunteers abandoned the effort by the hundreds, and railroads carried them home at half price. The movement dissolved, and Irish-American nationalism was forced to step back, take a hard look at itself, and regroup. *The New York Times* reflected popular sentiment when it stated that even if the Fenians had managed to take Canada, "No one believes it would produce the liberation of Ireland from British rule. It would be just as sensible to expect Russia to liberate Poland if she heard that our Polish fellow-citizens had overpowered the garrisons of Alaska."

The Fenians were the last Irish-American nationalist movement to capture the enthusiasm and support of such a large segment of the Irish community in the United States. Unlike these Famine immigrants, whose love for the homeland and hatred of the British were rooted in direct personal experience, later Irish-American nationalists often seemed less intent on freeing Ireland from British rule than on silencing the attacks of prejudiced American nativists and enhancing Irish-American prestige. Many agreed with Thomas Francis Meagher when he insisted in New York's *Irish News* that the liberation of Ireland was a necessary precondition if her exiled children ever hoped to be 'honored or respected'.

There was no doubt, though, that the Fenians had made a deep impression on the mind of America. Their activities were widely covered by the press, and when it was all over, President Grant signed a general pardon for anyone who had participated in the invasions. During a visit to St. Louis he was presented with a petition to free Captain O'Neill that ended with two columns of signatures ten feet long. Even the English freed their Fenian prisoners. When five of them arrived in New York in January 1871, the U.S. Congress voted 172 to 21 for a resolution extending 'a cordial welcome to the capital, also to the country'. Republicans and Democrats competed to see who could be the first to meet their ship, the steamer *Cuba,* and the city mounted lavish parades and receptions to welcome them.

If Irish-Americans were willing to fight to free Ireland from its detested union with England, however, they were equally ready to fight to preserve the American Union, and distinguished themselves by their courage in armed combat after the Civil War was declared in 1861. Thousands of Irish and Irish-Americans had already fought in the Mexican War, under such outstanding Irish-American officers as General William O. Butler, commander-in-chief of the army in Mexico, General S. W. Kearny, who directed the conquest of California, and General James Shields, who commanded militia forces and went on to lead a division during the Civil War. Now, even though their own battles for acceptance and equality were far from over, they rallied overwhelmingly to the cause of the Union, and proved once and for all that they deserved to be respected as full-fledged and loyal citizens of their adopted country. When Confederate troops attacked Fort Sumter, Irish Americans rushed to answer President Lincoln's appeal for volunteers. Only 11 days later,

CHAPTER FOUR

LEFT *Union Brigadier General Thomas W. Sweeny fought bravely in many campaigns of the Civil War, including Shiloh and Corinth. As was common at the time, a popular march was named for him. Sweeny later achieved a different sort of fame as a leader of the Fenian invasion of Canada in 1866.*

on April 23, 1861, a thousand men had been picked from the 6,000 who applied and 'The Fighting 69th' — the most famous of all the Irish regiments — marched through New York City on their way south to defend Washington. In all, as many as 150,000 Unions soldiers were Irish-born — up to 51,000– from New York State alone — and thousands more were of Irish parentage. No fewer than 38 Union regiments were officially designated 'Irish'. Exclusively Irish regiments were formed in Massachusetts, Michigan, Ohio, Indiana, Illinois and Iowa.

These Irish-Americans fought and died to demonstrate their loyalty and love for their new homeland. "To live on her soil, to work for the public good, and die in the country's service, are genuine aspirations of the Son or Erin," British consul Thomas Grattan wrote from Boston in 1859. But many recruits saw the war against the secessionist South as a war against their ancient enemy, England, as well, a war to preserve the rights and power of the people's democracy against southern aristocrats *and* British monarchists. The English were natural allies of the Confederacy because they needed the cotton from Southern plantations to supply their textile mills. Recruiters for Irish regiments dramatized this connection by printing up posters declaring that the 'cotton lords and traitor allies of England must be put down'. Loyal Fenian supporters often joined up to get training for the coming struggle for Irish liberation, and some hoped that England's alliance with the South would mean a direct military confrontation before the present war was over.

The hoped-for confrontation with England never came, but the Union's Irish-American regiments were involved in more than their share of fierce face-offs against the soldiers of the Confederacy. On the battlefield the Irish won acclaim for their fighting spirit and bravery, if not for their discipline, and many Confederate officers considered them the best soldiers in the Union army. One war correspondent wrote that the Irish 69th Regiment 'fought like tigers' in the first Battle of Bull Run.

Those thousand hand-picked men of the 69th were led by Colonel Michael Corcoran as they marched to the steamer that would carry them to Washington. Corcoran had become a hero of the American Irish community a year earlier when

he refused to send his regiment to parade before the visiting Prince of Wales. He was court-martialed and relieved of his command, but was reappointed when the war broke out and Captain Thomas Meagher, one of the exiled 'men of '48', was named as his aide. Despite his British accent and bearing, products of his British schooling, Meagher was idolized by the American Irish and was promoted to brigadier general by the war's end. He was known as 'Meagher of the Sword' after a speech he had made during the '48 uprising, urging his fellow countrymen to "grasp the sword and strike for freedom."

Two Union charges had already been beaten back by a withering hail of Confederate gunfire when General William Tecumseh Sherman called on the Irish to throw themselves into the fight at Bull Run, and it was there that they began to earn the right to be called 'The Fighting 69th'. The entire regiment knelt with their bayonets gleaming and green flag flying above them as their priest, Father O'Reilly, blessed them and commended each soul to God. Then the men rose,

BELOW LEFT *General William Orlando Butler (1791–1880) was one of many Irish Americans to find a distinguished career in the military. Butler served in the Mexican War, and fought for the North in the Civil War.*

put on their caps, and Captain Meagher cried out to them, "Come on, boys, you've got your chance at last!"

The 69th — and other Irish regiments — paid dearly for that long-awaited chance to be called Americans. The battlefields of the Civil War became the melting pot that made all soldiers, foreign and native-born, comrades in arms. One Irish color-bearer named Mike Scannel of the 19th Massachusetts Regiment recalled his surprise when a group of Confederate soldiers surrounded him and ordered, "Hand over those colors, Yankee". "Yankee is it now," he said, as he gave them the flag. "Faith I've been twenty years in this country and nobody ever paid me the compliment before."

The 'Fighting 69th' answered Meagher's challenge. Stripping to their shirtsleeves, even barefoot in the searing July heat, and carrying only their guns and ammunition, the men raced toward a hill that was occupied by Confederate artillery, past groves of trees where enemy riflemen lay concealed. They raised a battle cry — part-

English, part-Gaelic — that would become as famous as the Rebel yell. Three times they charged, aiming their bayonets at Confederate cavalry, and three times they were driven back.

At one point Colonel Corcoran ordered the flag-bearer to lower the green regimental flag, which had become a target for Confederate bullets. The soldier insisted on keeping it upright, and was killed moments later. Another man jumped up to raise the colors and he, too, was immediately shot down. One color-bearer in Meagher's company, named John Keefe, shot a Confederate soldier after the man had grabbed the flag from him, but was dragged down by a group of rebel soldiers and taken prisoner. Pulling out a gun that he had hidden in his shirt, he rescued the flag and carried it back to the Union line, amid cheers from his fellow Irishmen.

The volunteers of the 69th who survived Bull Run served out what remained of their 90-day enlistment period, but many rejoined the regiment when Meagher, now a colonel, was given permission to form an Irish Brigade that was originally made up of the 69th, the 88th, and the 63rd New York Volunteers. While on a recruiting visit to Boston in September 1861, just two months after the regiment had suffered such heavy losses at Bull Run, Meagher declared that "the Irish soldier will henceforth take his stand proudly by the side of the native-born, and will not fear to look him straight and sternly in the face, and tell him that he has been equal to him in his allegiance to the Constitution". By facing the Confederate army in battle, and doing their duty bravely, these Irish had also faced down their old enemies, the nativists, and there could no longer be any doubt that they deserved to be called Americans.

All the Irish units proudly affirmed their origins and identity. When Meagher's Irish Brigade set off to join the Union army in Virginia, it marched under a green banner that bore an Irish harp, sunburst and wreath of shamrocks along with their motto, which proclaimed in Gaelic, 'They shall never retreat from the charge of lances'. The slogan of the Massachusetts 28th, emblazoned in Gaelic on their flag beside an Irish harp, was 'Clear the Road'. The state's 'Irish Ninth' took as its motto 'As allies and strangers thou didst us befriend. As sons and true patriots we do thee

CHAPTER FOUR

RIGHT *The Irish volunteered with enthusiasm for the Civil War. Dozens of Irish regiments were formed. This recruiting poster appeared in Boston in 1861, urging men to join and emulate "the glory of the other Irish regiments."*

BELOW RIGHT *Stephen Douglas is remembered today as Lincoln's opponent in the presidential race of 1860, but in the 1850s he was an Irish hero. As the Democratic candidate he received very strong Irish support.*

ABOVE CENTER *President Abraham Lincoln visited victorious Major General George G. McClennan after the Battle of Antietam in 1862. McClennan is sixth from left; George Armstrong Custer stands just to the left of Lincoln.*

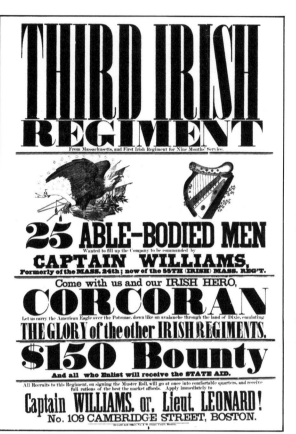

CHAPTER FOUR

LEFT *This recruiting poster of 1862 used shamrocks, Irish harps and the heroic name of Colonel Michael Corcoran, head of the famed 69th Regiment, to attract men to an Irish regiment forming in New York.*

BELOW LEFT *Although Major General Irwin McDowell was defeated by the Confederates at the first battle of Bull Run, he went on to achieve victory in later fights.*

BELOW CENTER *A Catholic chaplain conducts mass for the 69th New York State Militia encamped at Fort Corcoran, Washington D.C., 1861. The photographer is Mathew Brady.*

CHAPTER FOUR

RIGHT *The 69th New York Regiment, "The Fighting Irish", march off to the Civil War on April 23, 1861, from the original St. Patrick's Cathedral on Prince and Mott Streets in New York City. The most famous of the many Irish regiments that fought in the war, the 69th went on to achieve distinction in World War I and World War II.*

defend'. Other noted Irish units included New York's Fire Zouaves, recruited from the city's predominantly Irish fire companies, Brooklyn's Irish 113th, the 37th New York Volunteers, or 'Irish Rifles', who were sponsored by Tammany Hall, and the 23rd Illinois Infantry, known as 'Mulligan's Brigade' after its leader, Colonel James A. Mulligan.

Irish troops were consistently among the first to fight, and each Irish-American community eagerly followed its men's achievements in battle. The most famous Irish corps of all, however, was the Irish Brigade.

The Brigade's first major encounter with rebel troops came at Fair Oaks, a railroad station six miles east of Richmond, on May 31, 1862. The Union army was pushing toward the Confederate capital, but two Union charges had already been beaten back when General Edwin 'Old Bull' Sumner approached his Irish soldiers on horseback, took off his hat and gave what one observer called "probably the only [speech] of the old hero's life". He told the brigade that unless they could win it the battle was lost. "I'll go my stars on you," he said, pointing to his jacket. "I want to see how Irishmen fight, and when you run, I'll run too."

The Brigade let loose a loud cheer and advanced into the woods with determined steps. There was a loud volley when they attacked and then continuous rifle fire. Suddenly a cheer arose and a soldier rode up to order the artillery to follow their advancing comrades; the battle was won, and General Sumner was an ardent admirer of the Irish Brigade from then on.

Their greatest victory came, however, the following September at Antietam. Union forces managed to halt the Confederate invasion of Maryland and Pennsylvania, but the fierce fighting left 23,000 dead or wounded on both sides — more than on any other single day of the war. The Irish were almost swallowed up in the action as they drove the rebels back beyond a sunken road that was strewn with dead bodies from an earlier exchange of artillery fire. Once they had taken it, the Brigade used the depression as a defense and held it to the end, but one regiment lost nearly 50 percent of its men and another lost more than 30 percent. One witness reported that the rebels seemed to view the green flag with particular malice, and shot down five of the Brigade's color-bearers, one after another, in less than five minutes; a total of fifteen were killed in that one day alone.

When the fifth man fell, even these brave soldiers hesitated, but then 'Big Gleason', the 63rd's captain, rose to his full six feet seven inches, rushed forward and picked up the flag. Moments later a bullet shattered the staff, but he wrapped the flag around his body, cinched his sword belt on top of it, and finished the fight unscathed.

Meagher, who had by now been promoted to general, led the Brigade up a hill into enemy fire. They met first one line of rebel rifles and then a second, three feet below the surrounding surface, but despite a heavy rain of bullets they carried out Meagher's order to tear down a rail fence that had been sheltering enemy riflemen and then engaged a large force of infantry. The general's horse was shot out from under him and a bullet tore a hole in his uniform; the flag was shot down 16 times, and each time a man rushed in to save it. The battle raged for over four hours, but in the end the Confederate troops were beaten back. The Brigade's 69th Regiment had lost 169 of 317 men in the front lines.

That December, at Fredericksburg, after signing up new recruits, the Brigade was ordered to attack an impregnable Confederate position on Marye's Heights. Meagher urged them on as "fellow exiles of Erin," and told them to fasten a sprig of evergreen in their caps to replace their green flags, which had been ravaged by enemy volleys. As they charged again and again, savage rifle fire reduced one regiment of 700 men to 150; of their five regiments, only 200 men remained. The 'Fighting 69th' lost 128 out of a corps of 238.

When the Brigade were finally forced to retreat, "the hillsides [were] for acres strewn with their corpses thick as autumnal leaves," reported the war correspondent for the *London Times*. "After witnessing the gallantry and devotion exhibited by Meagher's troops," he wrote, "the spectator can remember nothing but their desperate courage." He called the grim scene "the best evidence of what manner of men they were who pressed on to death with the dauntlessness of a race which has gained glory on a thousand battlefields, and never more richly deserved it then at the foot of Marye's Heights on the 13th day of December, 1862". Even Confederate General Robert E. Lee honored them with the judgment

CHAPTER FOUR

LEFT *Brigadier-general Philip Kearny (1815–1862) was a notable Union officer in the Civil War. He served with distinction under General McClennan and was killed in action at the second battle of Bull Run.*

FAR LEFT *A hero of the Irish Revolution of 1848 (and designer of the Irish flag), Thomas Francis Meagher came to America and became the commander of the Irish Brigade, consisting of the famed 69th Regiment and two others, in 1861. He is shown here in the uniform of the Irish Zouaves.*

that "never were men so brave. They ennobled their race by their splendid gallantry on that desperate occasion. Though totally routed, they reaped a harvest of glory. Their brilliant, though hopeless, assaults on our lines excited the hearty applause of our officers and soldiers." After the battle of Chancellorsville, which was soon to follow, only 520 men remained out of the Brigade's entire five regiments.

When the decisive battle of the war was fought the next summer at Gettysburg, the Irish Brigade once again upheld its reputation for courage and daring. It fought heroically and sustained heavy losses.

Irish-Americans served with distinction on the side of the Confederacy as well; up to 40,000 of its troops were Irish-born, and perhaps an equal number were of Irish descent. Alabama had its Emerald Guards, South Carolina its Emerald Light Infantry and Virginia its Emmet Guards. General Lee called Patrick Cleburne, the most famous Irish general in his army, "a dashing military man" who "was all virtue" and who had "inherited the intrepidity of his race".

Other celebrated generals on the Union side included Philip Sheridan, the son of Irish immigrants, who as a tactician was the equal of Generals Grant and Sherman. Dashing and colorful, he is especially remembered for his 20-mile gallop from Winchester to rally his troops in the Shenandoah Valley. Irish-born Brevet Brigadier General James Rowan O'Beirne of the 37th New York Volunteers — 'The Irish Rifles' — was wounded many times and was awarded the Congressional Medal of Honor for his valor. After the war, as Provost Marshall in Washington, he directed the pursuit and capture of the men who assassinated President Lincoln. O'Beirne was later appointed United States Commissioner of Immigration and New York City Commissioner of Charities.

Although the bravery and self-sacrifice of Irish-American officers and enlisted men was of incalculable importance in winning the war for the Union, the Irish contributed to the war effort in other ways as well. Irish-American priests followed their troops onto the battlefields and said Mass before each engagement and every Sunday. Irish-American nuns nursed the wounded. A Dublin-born Irishman and band leader, Patrick Gilmore, wrote the lyrics to what became perhaps the most famous song of the era, 'When Johnny Comes Marching Home', after leaving Ireland at 19 to avoid entering the priesthood. And Matthew Brady, the son of immigrants and in his day the nation's most noted photographer, visited the battle-grounds of the war with his assistant, Timothy Sullivan, and recorded for history the lives and valiant deaths of ordinary Civil War soldiers, many of them Irish-Americans like himself. Brady had left his parents' farm in upstate New York in 1890 to work in New York City, where he studied the infant art of photography and later opened his famous photo gallery, the 'Broadway Valhalla'.

When the war broke out in 1861, Archbishop Hughes of New York had strongly supported the

CHAPTER FOUR

RIGHT *Confederate General Patrick Cleburne served with distinction at Missionary Ridge, Chickamauga, Chattanooga and elsewhere. His division was known for its fighting spirit.*

BELOW RIGHT *Major-general Benjamin F. Kelley served under General McClennan in the Civil War. Union troops under his command routed the Confederates at the Battle of Phillipi in West Virginia in 1861.*

BENJAMIN F. KELLEY,
MAJOR-GENERAL U. S. VOL.

Union, but his attitude toward abolition and abolitionists was just the opposite: "We despise, in the name of all Catholics," he declared, "the 'Idea' of making this war subservient to the philanthropic nonsense of abolitionism." The Irish were "willing to fight to the death," he said, "for the support of the constitution, the government, and the laws of the country," but they would not fight for the abolition of slavery. Private Peter Casey revealed the basis for this hostility when he complained in a letter that anti-Irish prejudice was still rampant in non-Irish army units, and that despite the North's desire to free the slaves, "they will not give us a chance . . . the Negro and not the welfare of the Country is what most Engrosses their minds and perhaps when all is over they will turn their attention to the burning of Convents and Churches as the[y] have done before . . . the enemies of our Race and Religion are numerous every where yet". The Irish had no desire to fight to free the slaves when they saw themselves still oppressed and persecuted in the land of liberty and equality. Thus, when President Lincoln issued the Emancipation Proclamation in the fall of 1862, Irish-Americans felt betrayed. It was a different war now, with a different purpose than the one they had supported so valiantly.

CHAPTER FOUR

LEFT *General Philip Henry Sheridan (1831–1888) was a famed cavalry officer. His charge at Missionary Ridge in 1863 was crucial to the Union victory there. In April 1865 he cut off the Confederate retreat at Appomattox and forced Lee to surrender.*
CENTER LEFT
"Sheridan's Ride" has gone down in Civil War history as an outstanding example of leadership. Union General Phil Sheridan (1831–1888) was surprised by a counter-attack at Cedar Creek; he rode to the battle-field, rallied his troops and won a decisive victory.

Irish laborers had long been competing with free blacks for jobs, and tension between the two groups grew when black scabs were brought in to break a strike led by Irish longshoremen in April 1863. Then on July 11 in New York City the first names were drawn for the new draft.

It was already apparent by the second year of the war that the North needed more soldiers than it could enlist as volunteers. A draft law was passed on March 3, 1863, which made men between 20 and 45 eligible for conscription. The only exemptions were granted to those who could pay $300 or find a substitute. Because most Irish could not afford to buy their way out of the draft, the burden fell unequally on them, which was obvious when the names of the first draftees were announced. The lists were particularly upsetting to a community whose regiments had already suffered heavy losses in the war, and they set off four days of the worst rioting in the nation's history. Angry Irish mobs looted and burned the draft office, fashionable homes and then the Colored Orphan Asylum. They beat, shot and lynched any blacks they could find, and despite pleas from the Catholic clergy and attempts by police — many of them Irish, as well — the violence did not end until troops were sent in and Archbishop John

Hughes used his influence as leader of the Irish community to calm the rioters. Addressing a huge crowd from the balcony of his residence, he begged them to keep the peace, and ended by saying:

I know that, under the misguidance of real or imaginery evils, people will sometimes get uneasy, and every man has his troubles, for I have my troubles, too; but I think with the poet that it is better to bear out slight inconveniences than to rush to evils that we have not yet witnessed ... When these so-called riots are over, and the blame is justly laid on Irish Catholics, I wish you to tell me in what country I could claim to be born? (Voices, "Ireland".) Yes, but what shall I say if these stories be true? Ireland, that has been the mother of heroes and poets, but never the mother of cowards. I thank you for your kindness and I hope nothing will occur until you return home, and if, by chance, as you go thither, you should meet a police officer or a military man, why, just look at him.

The famous Irish ferocity in battle had resurfaced on the streets of New York: estimates of the dead and wounded ranged from 300 to more than 1,200.

CHAPTER FOUR

RIGHT *Mathew Brady's Civil War photographs are now in the Library of Congress. He is shown here under fire with an artillery battery at Petersburg, Virginia in 1864. Brady is in the foreground wearing a straw hat.*

Two weeks later, *Harper's Weekly* tried to put the violence in perspective when it stated that

> *It must be remembered in palliation of the disgrace which, as Archbishop Hughes says, the riots of last week have heaped upon the Irish name, that in many wards of the city, the Irish were during the late riot staunch friends of law and order; that Irishmen helped to rescue the colored orphans in the asylum from the hands of the rioters; that a large proportion of the police, who behaved throughout the riot with the most exemplary gallantry, are Irishmen; that the Roman Catholic priesthood to a man used their influence on the side of the law, and that perhaps the most scathing rebuke administered to the riot was written by an Irishman — James T. Brady.*
>
> *It is important that this riot should teach us something more useful than a revival of Know-Nothing prejudices.*

Those old prejudices — against the Irish and against their religion — had clearly not vanished. But once the war was over, the nation was caught up in a vast outpouring of energy that shaped a new industrial landscape and sent thousands rushing west to make their fortunes. It was a wave that would carry the American Irish, too, to new places and new plateaus.

CHAPTER FOUR

BELOW LEFT *Born in 1823 of Irish parents in upstate New York, Mathew Brady was one of the nation's leading photographers before he was 30. He opened a studio in New York City and was famed as a portraitist, but it is through his Civil War photographs that he achieved lasting renown.*

ABOVE *James Shields came to America in 1826 from County Sligo at age 18. He served with distinction in the Mexican War and was later a Union general in the Civil War. He was active in the effort to bring Irish colonists to the Midwest; Shieldsville township in Minnesota is named for him.*

Chapter Five

WESTWARD HO!

*E*ven before the resurgent post-Civil War expansion began, thousands of Irish workers had joined America's first great push westward. The new nation had a lot of growing to do, but traveling through her untamed wilderness by horse or on foot was slow and arduous. It was Irish-American John O'Sullivan, the founding editor of the *Democratic Review* and later Minister to Portugal, who declared it America's 'manifest destiny' to extend her boundaries across the continent, and it was Irish-Americans who built the roads, canals and railroads that opened her vast heartland to farmers and other settlers.

The National Road through Pennsylvania and Ohio was a momentous undertaking that was completed under Irish contractors such as Philip McGinnis, Tully Gallager and Thomas Monaghan. The wages of six dollars a month drew more Irish workmen than could be hired.

As early as 1818 3,000 Irish were digging the Erie Canal in upper New York State, the nation's earliest and most famous canal. An enthusiastic supporter of the project, Governor DeWitt Clinton, was himself the grandson of an Irish immigrant. By 1826, the year after it was completed, over 5,000 Irish were working on four other major canals. Among those that employed large numbers of immigrants were New York State's Champlain, Black River and Chemung Feeder Canals, Pennsylvania's Chesapeake and Ohio, Connecticut's Enfield, Ohio's Miami and Rhode Island's Blackstone Canal. Irish-American journalist Thomas D'Arcy McGee would later write that the Irish supplied "the hands which led Lake Erie downwards to the sea, and wedded the strong Chesapeake to the gentle Delaware, and carried the roads of the East out to the farthest outpost of the West".

Boston, New York and New Orleans were major hiring centers for such projects, and some companies advertised in Ireland as well, where notices announced stunning rewards for workers that included 'meat three times a day, plenty of bread and vegetables, with a reasonable allowance of liquor, and eight, ten, or twelve dollars a month for wages'. For men eking out a living on impoverished farms, or subsisting as day laborers in crowded tenements, such offers were difficult to refuse, and they signed up by the hundreds.

Conditions on the job, however, did not usually match the glowing descriptions on the recruiting posters. A song called *Paddy on the Canal* told about an Irishman who liked both his work and his boss, a man who gave his gangs good whiskey and 'was father now unto us all'. The majority, however, were not so lucky. Labor contractors usually exploited their Irish recruits ruthlessly, well aware that there were always other 'Paddies' to take their places. Often they hired many more workers than the job required, just to drive wages down. Once on site the men put in long hours, from sunrise to sunset, at hard, dangerous jobs; canal laborers cleared forests and used pick and shovel to dig through mosquito-infested swamps. Accidents and disease killed many canal diggers, who often stood knee-deep in water — close to 20,000 deaths were recorded in a verse about a new canal that was published in the New Orleans *Times Picayune* on July 18, 1837:

> Ten thousand Micks, they swung their picks,
>   To dig the New Canal
> But the choleray was stronger 'n they,
>   An' twice it killed them awl.

When payday arrived, contractors often charged outrageous prices for supplies at outlying camps, or paid in overpriced merchandise when they paid at all. Wages averaged ten to fifteen dollars a month and only five dollars a month during the winter, with no compensation for time missed because of illness. Whiskey was part of canal workers' pay and drunkenness and brawling, especially after payday, were the frequent result. Fights would erupt between gangs whose rivalries dated back to the old country, or between Irish workers and other laborers who were competing for their jobs. Much of the unrest was no doubt a response to the miserable, backbreaking toil they faced daily, perhaps even an unorganized kind of protest.

Living conditions for the 'canalers' and their families were equally bad. Home was usually either a tent or a board-and-sod shanty thrown up as quickly as possible and abandoned as the work site shifted. Missionary priests visited the camps to celebrate Mass and baptize the children, and the men contributed what they could from their meager earnings to build rude churches along the route. Many laborers were forced to leave their wives and children in the city, however, and wives who worked 12-hour shifts in factories or as domestics often found it very hard to hold the family together.

No sooner were the new roadways and canals completed than a great era of railroad building began — and once again, it was the Irish who built them. Starting in the 1830s, labor gangs went to work putting down track in New York, Pennsylvania, Ohio, Illinois, Iowa, Wisconsin and Georgia. From 1840 on they laid most of the 30,000 miles that ran from New York to Chicago by 1856 and to St. Louis by 1860. They endured the same long hours and low pay as canal workers, and their jobs were at least as dangerous — a popular saying claimed that there was "an Irishman buried under every tie". When the roadbed sliced through hills or mountains, groups were lowered in straw baskets to set and ignite sticks of dynamite and then were hurriedly drawn up again — but not always fast enough. Many were crushed by collapsing embankments before the blast could go off, or buried in cave-ins. After reading about an Irish worker's accidental death in 1836, another Irishman protested angrily: "How often do we see such paragraphs in the paper as an Irishman drowned — an Irishman crushed by a beam — an Irishman suffocated in a pit — an Irishman blown to atoms by a steam engine — ten, twenty Irishmen buried alive by the sinking of a bank — and other like casualties and perils to which honest Pat is constantly exposed in the hards toils for his daily bread?"

For many of the men it was all too true, as the song *Pat Works on the Railway* claimed that "In eighteen hundred and forty-five/I found myself more dead than alive/From working on the railway". And the next verse went on to suggest how railway workers were treated:

It's "Pat do this" and "Pat do that,"
Without a stocking or cravat,
Nothing but an old straw hat
While I worked on the railway.

An immigrant who had spent 12 years on railroad gangs bitterly described his existence in a letter he wrote home to Ireland in 1860: "It would take more than a mere letter to tell you the despicable, humiliating, slavish life of an Irish laborer on a railroad in the States. I believe I can come very near it by saying that everything, good and bad, black and white, is against him; no love for him — no protection in life; can be shot down, run through, kicked, cuffed, spat on; and no redress, but a response of, 'Served the damn son of an Irish b—— right, damn him'."

Dubliner Charles Locke painted an equally sober picture of his life as a teamster for Canadian railroad contractors, for which he got to keep 12 dollars a month after his board was paid: "I am up at four a clock every morning out and feed my

teems then to breakfast and off to the working ground it is mostly eight O Clock before my worke is over [and] I am often so tired that I wish God in his mercy would take me to himself."

Life in the labor camps provided little relief. Workers often stayed in boardinghouses run by the contractors, where they had to climb a ladder outside to reach their crowded sleeping spaces. Others lived in the same kind of board huts that had housed canal workers. One observer in upstate New York in 1860 described "the fierce wind howling through" such a shanty, which was occupied by an Irish railroad worker and his family. All five lacked "sufficient clothing to protect them against the terrible climate", and although they kept a fire burning inside, a "vessel filled with water the night before . . . though within four feet of the fire . . . was frozen solid".

The compensation for enduring such conditions was low by almost any standards. The Connecticut Railroad paid laborers 70 cents a day in 1848, and the men struck for a 15-cent raise. The Illinois Central advertised impressive wages of $1.25 a day and good board for two dollars a week, but the reality was often very different from the picture painted by recruiting posters. A worker's daily whiskey ration was a pint and a half, dispensed in nine separate portions, and the men drank it freely to ward off cholera, but it also ignited many already dangerously restive hot tempers. When Irish-Americans built the Erie Railroad through New York State in 1847, warfare broke out between rival Corkonian and Far Downer workers, and after the triumphant Far Downers challenged a German crew, the rioting grew so fierce that the state militia was called in and remained on duty nearby for a month.

Not every worker was unhappy with his life on the railroad, however. Michael Byrne, a very poor and illiterate Irish speaker from a village in County Galway, dictated a letter to the Crown official who had organized the emigration of 253 impoverished peasants to Canada in 1848. "Your Honour," he began, "I am now Employed in the rail road line earning 5s. a day . . . And instead of being chained with poverty in Boughill I am crowned with glory."

Certainly the feats of Irish railway workers merited such pride. Irish laborers built the Baltimore and Ohio, the Erie, the Illinois Central, the Western and Atlantic; they pushed the Wabash and the Chicago and Northwestern through Iowa, and the Western and Atlantic from Atlanta to Chattanooga. But by far their greatest achievement was the transcontinental railroad. Begun

CHAPTER FIVE

after the close of the Civil War in 1865, it ran from coast to coast and took 10,000 workers four years to complete. Many of the workmen were ex-soldiers, and they earned three dollars a day as tracklayers, graders, teamsters, clerks, black-smiths, masons and cooks. President Monroe's Indian 'removal policy' and President Jackson's 1830 Indian Removal Act had by then driven many eastern tribes westward, beyond the Mississippi, and railroad gangs had to keep their guns handy to protect themselves against Indians who fiercely resented such treatment and opposed this new intrusion on their grazing lands and traps. There were also fights with Chinese coolies, who were sometimes hired instead of Irish workers on western portions of the railroad. But on good days as much as a mile of track was laid down, and when the Union Pacific and the Central Pacific finally met at Promontory Point, Utah, on May 10, 1869, it was a triumphant moment for the overwhelmingly Irish construction crews. The son of one of those immigrant laborers, a former er-rand boy named William M. Jeffers, would later rise to become president of the Union Pacific from 1937 to 1946.

As they traveled west on canal and railroad crews, many Irish-Americans abandoned the crowded cities of the East altogether and created new towns, where they supported themselves and their families as shopkeepers, tradesmen or through a combination of farming and small in-dustry. Often they were able to buy land from the canal or railway company at very low prices. Rochester, like Buffalo, was largely a product of the Erie Canal, and it had its own Hibernian Benevolent Society by the 1830s. Woonsocket, Rhode Island, grew from the building of the Blackstone Canal, and nascent Irish communities sprang up in Pawtucket, Rhode Island, Lowell, Massachusetts, and elsewhere along the work routes. Railroad workers also established Irish settlements at almost every terminal and junc-tion, as well as in thriving urban centers like Chicago, St. Louis and Kansas City.

A number of western colonies were begun as farming communities by immigrants who came directly from Ireland, and these and other Irish settlers played an especially important role in helping Texas to gain its independence from Mexico and then its statehood. In 1828 James Power and James Hewitson brought 200 Irish families to Refugio, on the Gulf Coast, and John Mullen and Patrick McGloin accompanied another 300 families to neighboring San Patricio. Colonists who joined such groups could claim

4,428 acres for a 100-dollar fee, and the promoters were given much larger holdings. There was also a large Irish settlement at Galveston. One out-standing leader of the Texas independence movement was Thomas Jefferson Rusk, the son of an Irish immigrant stonemason. Rusk took part in the convention that declared the Mexican prov-ince an independent republic in 1835; ten years later he presided over another convention that backed its annexation to the United States. To-gether with Sam Houston, also a descendant of Irish immigrants, he was one of the first Texans elected to the United States Senate. A colony similar to these early Texas communities was or-ganized in Michigan by County Mayo–born fur-trader Charles O'Malley, who arranged for a substantial number of Mayo natives to settle there in 1834.

Later, after the flood tide of Famine immi-grants reached American shores, several promi-nent members of the Irish-American community urged their followers to move west on a much larger scale. The 1860 census showed that the majority of the 1,611,000 Irish in America still lived in the cities of New England, New Jersey, New York and Pennsylvania, and most were un-skilled. Writing about his travels among them, John Francis Maguire spoke of "the evils of re-maining in the great cities", and an 1855 editorial in the widely read Irish-American newspaper, *The Citizen,* urged

> *Westward Ho! The great mistake that emi-grants, particularly Irish emigrants, make, on arriving in this country, is, that they re-main in New York, and other Atlantic cities, till they are ruined, instead of proceeding at once to the Western country, where a virgin soil, teeming with plenty, invites them to its bosom . . . Had they continued their journey westward, without halting, many of them would be now enjoying the happiness of inde-pendence . . . Their children would revel in the glories and grandeurs of nature . . .*
>
> *What then is the duty of the unemployed or badly paid emigrants residing in New York, Philadelphia and Boston? To start at once for the West.*

That same year Thomas D'Arcy McGee, deeply troubled by the situation of his countrymen in Irish towns along the Atlantic seaboard, tried to organize a new, large-scale program to plant Irish colonies out West. He asked the immigrants:

LEFT *The father of the state of Texas, Sam Houston was born in 1793. He entered politics and became a Congressman from Tennessee; he was later Governor of the state. In 1829 he moved to Texas, then a part of Mexico. He commanded at the battle of San Jacinto in 1836 that defeated the Mexicans. Houston then became the first president of the Republic of Texas. After Texas joined the United States, he was Senator and then Governor. Houston opposed secession and was forced to resign in 1861; he died in 1863.*

In the villages of New England
Are you happy, we would know?
Are you welcome, are you trusted?
Are you not? Then Rise and Go!

General James Shields, a native of County Tyrone and a distinguished veteran of the Mexican War and later of the Civil War, was another leader of the Go West movement. He served as governor of the Oregon Territory in 1848 and as U.S. Senator from Illinois after that. In 1855 he founded an Irish farming colony in Minnesota that by 1857 included a Catholic church and school. Towns bearing the names Shieldsville, Erin, Montgomery and Kilkenny testify to his legacy. Several other such farming colonies were begun in Minnesota as late as the 1880s.

Catholic bishops in western states soon joined the crusade to lure the Irish from their urban communities, in order to give them a chance at a better life, to spread the Catholic faith throughout the country — and to enlarge their own pastoral flocks. In the forefront of the crusade were

CHAPTER FIVE

Archbishop John Ireland of St. Paul and Bishop John Lancaster Spalding of Peoria, as well as churchmen in Wisconsin, Iowa, Nebraska and South Dakota. Minnesota hailed its bountiful potato crop, and Wisconsin compared its lakes and fields to Ireland's while claiming that its butter was superior.

An even more influential voice, however, opposed these new colonization schemes. New York's first archbishop, John Hughes, considered McGee a dangerous radical, and he used his tremendous popularity among Irish Catholics to dissuade them from joining any mass exodus. In a dramatic counterattack on the Go West movement he attended a public meeting incognito on March 26, 1857, and after standing to speak revealed his identity and then harshly condemned the campaign.

Hughes believed the organizers were in fact saying to their countrymen "Go you. We stay". He felt strongly that the Irish did not have the skills necessary to farm the American frontier; they had never cut logs or guided a plough, and they did not have the funds to travel west and support themselves until they could learn. His critics suggested that the archbishop simply did not want to lose parishioners and revenue.

Bishop Spalding regretted Archbishop Hughes's position, and declared that "no other man could have done so much to convince [Irish Catholics] that their interests for time and eternity required that they should make homes for themselves on the land". Thomas D'Arcy McGee, disillusioned by his feud with Archbishop Hughes and the failure of his resettlement attempts, moved to Canada and became a leader in the Confederation movement there. James Shields went on to serve as a senator from Minnesota and then from Misouri — the only man ever to represent three different states in the United States Senate. Even as late as the 1870s only eight in every hundred Irish-Americans was a farmer. Recalling the emigrants' bitter experiences in their homeland, some observers have maintained that "the Irish rejected the land because the land had rejected them".

The small number who did establish farms in fertile new areas, though, or found other jobs in the growing cities and towns of the Midwest and West, often achieved a degree of acceptance and prosperity that their urban brothers and sisters back East would not equal for many years to come. The frontier was a wide-open, classless society where the new settlers adapted more easily to regional values and could be judged for their accomplishments alone. Irish farmers were known and welcomed for their generosity and willingness to help their neighbors. A number of them seemed to enjoy taming the land, starting a successful farm, and then selling it and moving on to begin again somewhere else. Even before the Civil War, the Irish had spread so far west that St. Patrick's Day was celebrated from New York to San Francisco, and in between at places as widely scattered as Pottsville, Pennsylvania, Dubuque, Iowa, and Madison, Wisconsin. Heavily German Milwaukee even elected an Irish mayor, Edward O'Neill of Kilkenny, in 1863.

It was not farming but gold that lured thousands of Ireland's sons to California in the 1840s and 1850s, however. Even though many of them had to make the long, arduous journey from the East on steamers via Panama, the announcement that the precious metal had been discovered in the foothills of the Sierras sent a quarter of a million people rushing westward. Over $3 billion worth was finally found, but it made no one permanently rich. It did, however, make a boomtown of San Francisco practically overnight.

When gold fever struck in 1848, not long after U.S. troops defeated the Mexican army and forced Mexico to cede California to the United States, San Francisco was a sleepy Spanish village of 800 souls. Two years later California had become a state and the population of the city by the bay had hit 25,000 and was growing fast. It was a rough frontier town where "the rage for duelling, the passion for gambling and barefaced depravity prevail to a frightful degree", as missionary Father Eugene O'Connell reported in an 1853 letter to the head of his seminary in Dublin. The prospectors got there first, but right after them had come the con men and speculators, the shopkeepers and suppliers, the gamblers and saloonkeepers and ladies of less-than-impeccable virtue who inhabited the many 'temples to Venus' Father O'Connell also noted with regret. It was a town where the police force was so corrupt that citizens had to form their own vigilante groups to protect themselves.

A number of San Francisco's Irish soon took the lead in promoting the development of their adopted city, however, and some even made fortunes in the process. They were supported by a thriving Irish-American community whose members had first attended Mass in a wooden shanty in 1849 but had built a second Catholic church by 1853. The two were, Father O'Connell wrote, "crowded every Sunday". He also asked for more Irish priests. Less than 30 years later the Diocese

of San Francisco had 133 churches, 16 chapels, five colleges, five asylums, five hospitals and 128 priests serving 180,000 Catholics. By the 1860s, the community had its own ethnic newspapers, the *Irish News* and the *Irish People,* and by the 1870s it supplied a third of the city's police force and nine-tenths of its firemen.

One of San Francisco's first successful Irish-American businessmen was Peter Donahue. Dublin engineer James O'Farrel had settled in California in 1843, surveyed much of the city and laid out its streets, but it was Donahue who foresaw the need for a system of street lights. He set up a company, shipped in pipe from the East and coal from Wales to provide the gas, and inspired a city-wide celebration when the lights went on for the first time. Donahue also built the city's first iron foundry, ran a steamboat line, and founded the San Jose Railroad. His was one of the first mansions in downtown San Francisco, and for her trips about town he gave his wife, Anna, a coach made entirely of glass. Their daughter, Mary Ellen, married Baron Henry von Schroeder in a fashionable New York ceremony in 1883 — one of the first pairings of an American heiress with European nobility. When Peter Donahue died, his estate was valued at $4 million.

Mrs. Donahue's sister and brother also prospered. Her sister, Eleanor, married Edward Martin, who founded San Francisco's Hibernia Bank; his financial success assisted her social progress, and she remained the city's leading hostess into the 1890s. Her brother, John G.

Downey, had arrived from County Roscommon in 1849 with only ten dollars, opened a pharmacy in Los Angeles, and after entering politics was elected governor of the state in 1862 — just 13 years after he had arrived.

James Phelan of Queen's County was another Irishman who made his fortune in business. After landing in New York as a boy he worked in a grocery store, came to San Francisco after the gold strike, started a saloon and then went into real estate before opening his own bank. By 1870 he was one of the city's ten richest men, and he left an estate estimated at $7.5 million. His son, James Duval Phelan, was elected mayor of San Francisco and later served as a United States senator from 1915 to 1921.

An Irish-American who distinguished himself in government rather than business was David Broderick, who dabbled in several different occupations before moving to California during the Gold Rush. There he read law, was quickly elected to the state senate, became a leader in the Democratic Party and was elected a United States senator in 1855. Broderick was known for his honesty and directness, and he openly opposed the expansion of slavery into new territories and the Buchanan administration's Kansas policies. When he ran for re-election his enemies decided to try to get rid of him and one of his pro-Southern opponents challenged him to a duel. Broderick, not wanting to kill the man, fired into the ground, but his challenger shot him just below the heart. "They killed me," he said, dying, "because I was opposed to the extension of slavery and a corrupt administration."

Tom Maguire also traveled to California from New York with the Forty-Niners, and he put his experience tending bar in his old hometown to good use by opening the Parker House, the city's most luxurious saloon and gambling establishment. But his real love was the stage, and in 1850 he turned the top floor into the Jenny Lind Theater and gave San Francisco its first look at professional actors from back East. He went on to build two more theaters after the first one burned down; when the second proved too big to show a profit, he sold it to the city and it became the new City Hall. His third and final theater had its own resident acting company, and helped make Maguire the country's leading theatrical manager and promoter outside New York.

Thus while most of their countrymen remained in crowded and restrictive cities of the East, the San Francisco Irish, with similar backgrounds and experience, took full advantage of the West's

CHAPTER FIVE

LEFT *David Colbreth Broderick, born in Kilkenny in 1820, started his political career with Tammany Hall in New York City, but went to California with the gold rush of 1849. There he quickly rose in state politics and was elected to the U.S. Senate. An outspoken opponent of slavery, he was killed in a duel with a pro-Southern advocate in 1859. This photo is by Mathew Brady.*

CHAPTER FIVE

wider opportunities to advance to positions of power and prominence. They and their fellows throughout the state were so successful, in fact, that by the end of the century the California Irish were widely believed to have the 'Midas touch'. But of all those who made their mark there, few men did more to contribute to this reputation than the four who became known as the 'Silver Kings'.

It was two Irish miners, Peter O'Riley and Patrick McLaughlin, who in 1859 were working the site of a recent gold strike in the Sierras when they discovered the famous Comstock Lode, an incredibly rich vein of both gold and silver in western Nevada. It soon spawned the town of Virginia City, which quickly drew many more Irish and Yankees from California, as well as Welsh, Chinese, and other fortune hunters and camp followers. The two discoverers themselves lived the boom-and-bust scenario that typified the careers of many of these men. O'Riley sold his interest for $50,000, lost everything when he invested in mining stocks, and died in an insane asylum. McLaughlin also sold out for a fraction of the property's true value, and after spending lavishly, ended his days as a mining camp cook.

The rumors of still-undiscovered riches lingered in Virginia City, however, and the rumors traveled back to San Francisco with the miners. There James C. Flood and William S. O'Brien, two Irishmen from New York, ran a well-known waterfront saloon called the Auction Lunch Room specializing in fish chowder. They joined forces with two Irish friends, John Mackay and James Graham Fair, who were looking for financial backing to expand their search for the fabled lode. The fifth partner was James M. Walker, a rich Virginian. In March 1873 their persistence paid off when Mackay and Fair struck a vein of silver 50 feet wide — the largest single pocket of the metal ever unearthed — that ultimately produced ore worth over $500,000,000.

Walker quickly sold his one-fifth share in their bonanza to Mackay and returned to Virginia. O'Brien retired and lived quietly on his fortune until he died several years later. The remaining three, however, all used their enormous wealth to shape careers that were very different but equally impressive.

Jim Fair had been born in Belfast and moved to Chicago as a child before traveling west at the age of 18. He bought a mill in Nevada with his Comstock wealth and ruthlessly extended his control over Nevada development until he was elected a senator from that state by the Nevada legislature, but his achievements in Congress were less noteworthy than his business ventures had been. Both of his sons died tragically, one a suicide and one in an auto accident with his young bride after being disinherited by his father, who opposed the match. Fair's two daughters, however, successfully invaded New York society; Birdie married William K. Vanderbilt and Tessie married Herman Oelrichs, and both led the fashionable set that moved between summer residences in Newport and townhouses on Fifth Avenue.

James Flood almost immediately set out to put up a huge brownstone mansion atop Nob Hill, which was so well-built that it was one of the few structures left standing after the great earthquake and fire of 1906. He also erected a palatial home in suburban Menlo Park, whose many turrets and gables and all-white exterior prompted neighbors to christen it 'Flood's Wedding Cake'. Flood and his wife, a former chambermaid, were not embraced with alacrity by San Francisco society, but their beautiful daughter, Jennie, was the toast of the city and was courted by such desirable suitors as Ulysses S. Grant, Jr., the President's son, and a titled Englishman, Lord Beaumont.

The fourth member of the 'Irishtocracy', John William Mackay, was perhaps the most talented and also the most attractive: tall, good-looking, gentle and generous. Born into a poor family in Dublin in 1831, he arrived in New York in 1840 and worked as a shipyard apprentice there for several years. When the Gold Rush began he struck out for California, learned about mining as a pick-and-shovel man in Virginia City, became skilled at the job and was promoted to superintendent. Even as a laborer, though, he had taken part of his $4-a-day wages in company stock. When the Comstock Lode came in, his holdings made him a very rich man and financed his share of the firm that ultimately located the Bonanza.

Mackay had met his wife, a young widow named Louise Hungerford Bryant, in Virginia City when he was asked to contribute to a collection for her. She had been stranded there when her husband died, and the miners wanted to help her return to Canada with her infant daughter. John Mackay asked to meet Mrs. Bryant, fell in love and married her.

In 1874 the couple left Virginia City, where he had been the firm's managing partner, moved to San Francisco and then two years later to New York. Mackay formed the Commercial Cable Company, supported the laying of a transatlantic cable, beat out Jay Gould's Western Union monopoly against all odds, and turned down several nominations to the United States Senate. Although Mrs. Astor did not admit them to her social circle, their subsequent stay in Europe was a triumphant one. In Paris Mrs. Mackay hired a diplomat's wife as her social adviser, and by the time she moved to London the following year she was entertaining the Prince of Wales — the future King Edward VII — at her parties. He is said to have called John Mackay "the most unassuming American I have met", and despite their lack of education or 'breeding' the couple's innate Irish warmth, attractiveness and good manners made them friends wherever they went. Mrs. Mackay's daughter, Eva, later married the Italian Prince Fernando Galatro-Colonna.

John Mackay was as generous as he was unassuming, and even though most of the millions he gave away as anonymous gifts and loans went unrecorded, two notable exceptions stand as memorials to his magnanimity: the Mackay School of Mines at the University of Nevada and the Church of St. Mary's in the Mountains in Virginia City.

It was not only in California and Nevada that the adventurous Irish were making their fortunes in mining, however. Montana had extensive copper deposits and Colorado was rich in gold and silver. The large community of Irish-American miners in remote Butte, Montana, started a Robert Emmet Literary Association there, which fulfilled the Irish need for sociability as well as celebrating the wealth of their cultural heritage. Marcus Daly, a former telegraph messenger and farm laborer from County Cavan, earned vast sums from his Montana copper mines, which he consolidated into the Anaconda Silver Mine and the Anaconda Copper Mining Company, and was also a successful breeder of racehorses. The Maid of Erin Mine in desolate Leadville, Colorado, contained silver deposits that eventually produced great wealth for its hardy and hard-working Irish-American owners. Colorado gold and silver also made John Brown and his wife, Margaret Tobin Brown, fabulously wealthy and financed their magnificent home in Denver. But it was Margaret Brown's own Irish tenacity and cheerful courage that won her a secure place in history.

'Leadville Johnny' Brown came from a poor family and his wife had worked as a housemaid, but when Denver society rejected her because of her background she simply went off to Europe in the 1890s, learned five languages, and gave and attended social parties on the Continent. Return-

ing home in 1912 for one of her periodic visits, she was aboard the *Titanic* when it struck an iceberg and sank on its maiden voyage to the United States. Mrs. Brown escaped in Lifeboat Number 6 and, rowing through the night until her hands bled, she kept up the spirits of the other survivors by telling jokes and singing grand opera. After they were rescued 'Lady Margaret', as her shipmates called her, explained it as "typical Brown luck" and declared "I'm unsinkable". And thereafter she was known as 'the Unsinkable Mrs. Brown'.

Bravery was a trait displayed time and again by yet another group of Irishmen who left their mark on the American west, beginning in the 1840s. They were the soldiers, Indian fighters and cavalrymen who fought in the Mexican War, defended pioneers against Indian attacks on the expanding frontier and died with General Custer at the Little Bighorn. Like thousands of canal and railroad workers before them, many had arrived from Ireland in what had by the 1870s become a continuous stream of emigrants.

Myles Keogh was born in County Carlow in 1840 and fought with the Papal Army in Italy against Garibaldi's supporters before coming to America and being promoted to lieutenant-colonel during the Civil War. He became a soldier, he said, "to carry out at least some of the visionary fancies" that he and his brothers had "indulged in . . . days of long ago". He was made any army captain after the war ended and led a troop of the largely Irish 7th Cavalry in 1876 when they made their 'Last Stand' under General Custer against Crazy Horse and his braves.

Thomas Francis Meagher, the Civil War soldiers' 'Meagher of the Sword', also ended his days in the West. He was serving as acting governor of the Montana Territory in 1867 when, at the age of 44, he drowned in the Missouri River. The state later erected a statue at the capital in Helena to honor the fallen warrior.

A third figure who has become a legend among the Texas Irish in particular is Leander ('Lee') McNelly, the greatest of all Texas Ranger captains. McNelly imposed the rule of law on the murderers and cattle rustlers who held sway along the Rio Grande after the close of the Civil War. Slender, with a boyish face and mild blue eyes, he nonetheless possessed the firm will and quiet authority of a natural leader.

His parents were immigrants from County Down who died when Lee was still a boy, and he moved from what is now West Virginia to Texas with his older brother's family when he was 15.

CHAPTER FIVE

CHAPTER FIVE

Just shy of 17 when the Civil War began, he served for four years in the Confederate army, was promoted to captain and was several times decorated for bravery under fire.

As a Texas Ranger McNelly protected prisoners from lynching parties and the courts from outside disruption. He established a network of informers to help him control known criminals, and he and his men made frequent raids on saloons to scatter groups of troublemakers.

His greatest achievement, though, was crack-ing down on cattle rustlers who operated from bases in Mexico. When McNelly came to Nueces County in southwest Texas in 1875 up to 200,000 head of cattle a year were disappearing across the border, ranchers had formed their own posses, and criminals were taking advantage of the disorder to loot and pillage.

He immediately ordered the posses to disband, then tracked down a group of 12 employed by Mexican General Juan Cortinas, killed all of them and recaptured several hundred head of cattle. Finally, in a daring raid on the rustlers' headquarters three miles inside Mexico, McNelly ambushed and killed the chief of all the Rio Grande bandits, General Juan Flores, and forced the Mexicans to return the cattle they had stolen.

McNelly, Mackay and Margaret Brown are just a few of the Irish-Americans whose courage, tenacity and spirit of adventure helped to build the American west. There are thousands more whose names were never recorded. But by 1880 they and their countrymen had constructed the transportation systems that bound the nation together, dug millions of dollars in mineral wealth from its mountains, and helped settle and defend its western territories. At the same time their eastern brothers and sisters — the urban pioneers — were busy building, too, and the institutions they created would reach beyond the boundaries of race and ethnic loyalties and bring Americans together in ways that were different — but equally important.

MONUMENTS TO IRISH-AMERICAN ACHIEVEMENT

ABOVE *President William McKinley (1843–1901) in 1899.*

PAGES 82 AND 83 *The Hermitage, Andrew Jackson's home in Tennessee. The mansion is preserved and open to the public. It is filled with period furnishings and memorabilia of the President.*

ABOVE *This portrait of Chief Justice John Marshall was painted in
1832 by William J. Hubard. It hangs today in the National Portrait
Gallery in Washington, D.C.*

Emigrants to America today arrive by airplane, not ship, but from 1891 to 1975, Ellis Island in New York Harbor was where over two million Irish entered the country.

LEFT ABOVE *Leinster House in Dublin, where the Irish Parliament meets. The White House is modeled after the building.*

LEFT BELOW *Lock 17 on the New York State Barge Canal, otherwise known as the Erie Canal. Opened in 1825, the canal was built by the backbreaking labor of thousands of Irish immigrant workers.*

ABOVE *From 1886 until today, the Statue of Liberty in New York Harbor has welcomed immigrants from all over the world to America. By 1890, New York was called the greatest Irish city in the world. Today the estimated Irish-American population is over 13 million.*

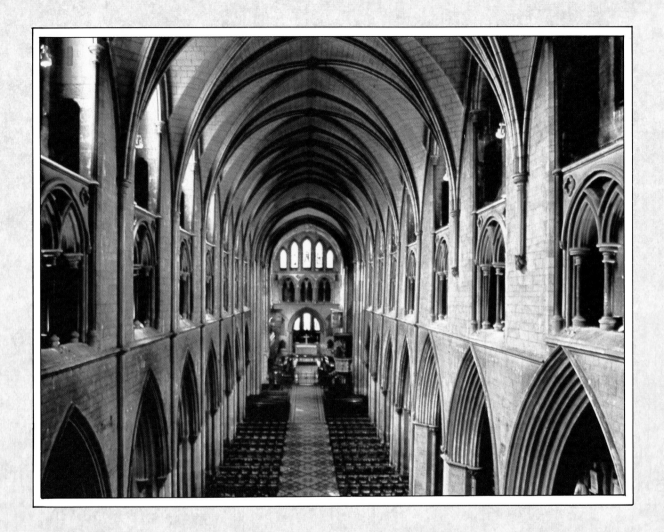

ABOVE *St. Patrick, the patron saint of Ireland, has a famed cathedral in Dublin, too. This interior shot shows the length of the church — at over 340 feet, it is the longest cathedral in Ireland.*

ABOVE *Notre Dame University in South Bend, Indiana — the symbol of Irish-Catholic higher education. The Notre Dame football team, the Fighting Irish, is a perennial contender for national acclaim.*

LEFT ABOVE *St. Patrick's Cathedral in Dublin was built between 1220 and 1254 and restored in the 19th century.*

LEFT *St. Patrick's Cathedral, a Gothic landmark in a sea of skyscrapers, is the most visible symbol of Irish-American pride.*

ABOVE *The modern library at Notre Dame University. The origins of the university are as much French as Irish, but the French role has been overwhelmed by the Irish in the popular view.*

ABOVE *The famed Dome at Notre Dame. This campus landmark is atop the main administration building.*

ABOVE *President Abraham Lincoln is honored by the Irish people with this bust and American flag in Phoenix Park, Dublin.*

LEFT ABOVE *Before the Civil War many Irish emigrants made for Baltimore. They helped build the city's largest Roman Catholic church, the Basilica of the Assumption.*

LEFT *Father Duffy Square, in the heart of Broadway's theater district, is named for the heroic Catholic chaplain of New York's Fighting 69th Regiment. A statue of Father Duffy adorns the square.*

ABOVE *William Jennings Bryan was the Democratic
candidate for President in 1900, and later served as Secretary
of State under President Woodrow Wilson. During his
presidential campaign he joined the Irish-American
community in condemning the nation's new imperialist
foreign policy, which many viewed as "a plant of English
growth."*

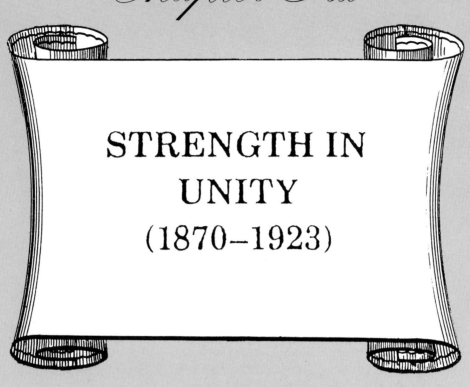

STRENGTH IN
UNITY
(1870–1923)

CHAPTER SIX

RIGHT ABOVE
*Sharpshooter Annie
Oakley (1860–1926)
rose from extreme
poverty to
international fame as
the star attraction of
Buffalo Bill's Wild
West Show from 1885
to 1902. She was
portrayed by Betty
Hutton in the hit
movie based on her
life,* Annie Get Your
Gun. *Buffalo Bill
otherwise known as
William Cody, was
also of Irish descent.*

RIGHT BELOW
*Immigrants to America
often entered the
country in New York.
This group in 1912 has
been processed at Ellis
Island in New York
Harbor and is awaiting
the ferry to Manhattan
and a new life.*

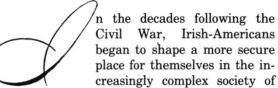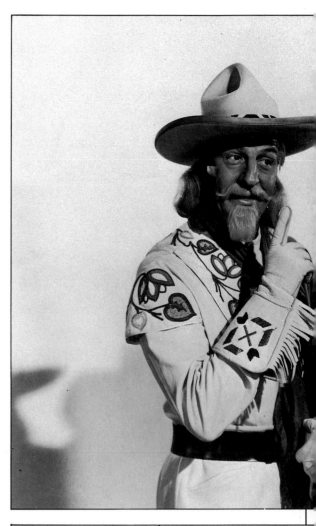

*I*n the decades following the Civil War, Irish-Americans began to shape a more secure place for themselves in the increasingly complex society of their adopted country. Emigration had become a way of life that sent an average of 50,000 'greenhorns' a year to the States, and the Irish-born population of the country peaked at 1.8 million in 1890. By 1900, first- and second-generation Irish-Americans totaled close to 5 million and outnumbered the population of Ireland itself. But even though the new arrivals were generally young, single Catholics with few skills and less capital, they were also more disciplined, thanks to changes in the Irish Catholic Church and the success of the temperance movement, and increasingly literate: by 1910, 97 percent could read and write English. Thus as a group they were more employable. The Irish-American newspapers that existed in almost every large city in the North and Midwest by the 1880s carried job listings and other information that eased the transition to a new way of life, and by now most of the newcomers also had relatives or friends who took them in, helped them find work and generally cushioned them from the harsh experiences of the Famine generation.

During the 1880s, too, Italians, Poles and other new immigrants started to take some of the lowest-level factory and mill jobs while the Irish began advancing to positions as foremen and supervisors or entering retailing and other entrepreneurial fields. Some became independent contractors or learned a skilled trade. As immigrants with more experience in the country, the Irish also acted as agents for the establishment, processing and policing the new foreign-born as customs officers and municipal clerks. After Irish emigration fell toward the end of the century, in response to government aid and long-overdue land legislation, female domestics were in even greater demand and could command higher wages. Daughters were educated as secretaries, teachers and nurses, and sons worked in the post office or took other municipal and civil service jobs. As a result, the children of immigrants began to buy homes for themselves and move out of the tenement neighborhoods where they had grown up. Some could purchase only small frame houses near the factories where they worked, but by the 1890s enough had joined the prosperous middle class to result in the term 'lace curtain' being coined to described them.

Local and family loyalties, though, generally

LEFT *On March 3, 1887, a 21-year-old girl, Anne Sullivan, the daughter of Irish immigrants, arrived at the Keller household in Alabama. Her job: to teach a blind and deaf seven-year-old named Helen. This photo of Helen and her beloved teacher was taken in 1894.*

remained strong. While a number of Irish-Americans found work in the iron and steel mills of Pittsburgh or Cleveland, the railroad yards of St. Louis or the stockyards and steelworks of Chicago, which was one-quarter Irish by 1900, the majority of city dwellers stayed in New York, Boston and Philadelphia, close to family and friends. But no matter where they were they dominated the fields of factory work, transportation and construction, and proudly put up the structures that gave their chosen city its modern face. Once Irish workers in New York had finished paving its streets, for example, they went on to build much of its urban transport system, including the Sixth and Ninth Avenue Els. They were largely responsible for constructing the Brooklyn Bridge, 'the eighth wonder of the world', between 1869 and 1883, even though the human cost was high; several riggers died when they fell from the massive cables that connected its 271-foot-high stone towers, and many other men were badly crippled from the 'bends' while they worked on the foundations in compressed-air caissons under the river bed. But it was an historic achievement, and the Irish were proud to be part of it. The Statue of Liberty was erected by Irish workingmen in 1886 after it arrived from France, and New York's first skyscrapers, including the famous Fuller or 'Flatiron' Building, were built primarily by Irish con-

CHAPTER SIX

RIGHT ABOVE *The Irish in the big cities often ended up working on the streetcars and trolleys. This famed photograph,* Terminal *by Alfred Stieglitz, was taken in New York City in 1892.*

RIGHT BELOW *In Pittsburgh, Irish workers pour a huge vat of molten steel into a mold at the Jones and Laughlin Steel Company in 1942.*

tractors and laborers.

By the late 1860s, however, Irish-Americans were starting to discover a larger identity and a wider sense of purpose in allegiances that extended beyond the local level. As their numbers increased and their understanding of their new country grew, they began to take on challenges that propelled them beyond the neighborhood, ward and parish and into positions of leadership and responsibility in labor unions, the Church and the Democratic Party. The Irish brought to all these roles their quick wit, human warmth and impressive skills in organizing and negotiating, and used them to mold institutions that would better serve their needs in a rapidly changing society.

For working people the most pressing needs were still a higher living standard and greater economic security. Ethnic associations like the Irish Catholic Benevolent Union (1869), the Catholic Total Abstinence Union (1872) and the Ancient Order of Hibernians (reorganized 1871) were working nationally for the social and financial betterment of Irish-Americans, but they dealt with the effects rather than the underlying cause of the problem. It was the almost limitless power of owners that kept workers from advancing, and the situation only worsened with the rapid industrialization that followed the Civil War.

As the post-war population grew and the market for consumer goods increased, industry required more steel for machine manufacturing and more coal to power the machines. Growing numbers of workers became dependent on large factories and mining companies for their livelihood, and the owners and managers naturally set terms of employment that favored their own interests — including low wages, long hours, and a lack of safety standards that left an estimated third of all workers the victims of crippling injuries. They could do so more easily because working people were divided among themselves: Irish against blacks, Germans against Irish, Irish against newer immigrants from southern and eastern Europe. These 'durty furruners' were deeply resented because they were willing to work for wages that the Irish, after decades of such treatment, felt were too low.

Drawing on their tradition of peasant 'combinations' and rural secret societies, Irish-Americans had organized laborers' associations and longshoremen's and quarrymen's societies even before the Civil War. They were also active in tailors', spinners' and shoemakers' unions in New England and New York. But when workers began to

realize that much remained to be done to secure their rights, the Irish were quick to take up the challenge. In 1861 Irishman Martin Burke helped to organize the American Miners Association, the first national union of coal miners, and set a precedent that was soon followed by many of his countrymen. Irish union leaders included J.P. McDonnell of the International Labor Union, James Larkin and James Connolly of the Industrial Workers of the World, William McLaughlin of the shoemakers' union and Denis Kearney of the California Workingmen's Party. In fact, until the Great Depression the fields that were most strongly unionized were consistently those with the largest number of Irish workers: the skilled trades, such as carpentry and plumbing, the longshoremen and the teamsters.

An Irish-American's natural assets as a union organizer included his length of time in the country relative to other immigrants and his command of the language. Terence Vincent Pow-

LEFT ABOVE *Many of the steelworkers who gave Pittsburgh the name "Iron City" were Irish. Their frame houses, with the smoke-shrouded city in the background, are photographed here around 1940.*

LEFT BELOW *The Irish who went West often ended in Chicago, where they worked in the stockyards, on the elevated trains, and in the traditional areas of police work and fire-fighting. This view, looking north from State and Washington streets, is typical for 1930.*

the Knights and announced its support for the rights of labor. Powderly was later appointed Commissioner of Immigration by President McKinley.

The miners that John Siney tried to unionize were among the most oppressed workers in the nation. During busy periods they might do fairly well, but during times when there was no work it was not unusual for a miner, who lived in dismal company housing and had to buy at company stores, to get a 'bobtail check' showing that he owed his employer money. Many were injured or killed while working; Siney addressed the diggers at the Avondale mine after more than 100 of their coworkers had been suffocated or burned to death in a fire. That most miners were Irish and the overseers and bosses primarily English, Scots and Welsh added ethnic animosity to class antagonism. When the miners' attempts to organize were ruthlessly repressed, they fought back by operating clandestinely. During the 1860s a group that called themselves the Molly Maguires was formed as a secret faction within the local lodges of the Ancient Order of Hibernians, and they soon earned a reputation for militant terrorism that tainted the labor movement for decades. Adopting the familiar methods of Irish agrarian violence, they brutalized and killed mine owners, torched buildings and intimidated voters at the polls. In the late 1870s, with much public fanfare and trumpeting, the leaders were tried and found guilty of nine murders; 20 Mollies were executed. The witness whose testimony convicted them was James McParlan, a charming, genial Irishman and Pinkerton agent who had penetrated the organization. The leading prosecutor, Franklin B. Gowan, was the son of Irish immigrants, a successful lawyer, railroad executive and mine operator, and an implacable enemy of labor's attempts to organize. Thomas Ainge Devyr, another Irishman and champion of many liberal causes, condemned the hangings as 'judicial murder'.

The Molly Maguires were crushed, but their revolt dramatized the need for labor to organize. By 1901 miners were among the largest groups in the American Federation of Labor, which was founded in 1886 and quickly succeeded the more loosely structured Knights of Labor after the Chicago Haymarket bombing and ensuing riot temporarily demoralized the union movement. At the turn of the century three-quarters of the nation's unionized workers were AF of L members. Many of the 25 craft unions that formed the federation were Irish-led, and one of its founders, Peter McGuire, is known as the 'Father of Labor

derly, the son of Irish parents, was so affected by a speech John Siney gave in 1869 while trying to organize Irish miners in Pennsylvania that he insisted one "could see Christ" in Siney's face and in his words "hear a new Sermon on the Mount". A machinist and former mayor of Scranton whose father had emigrated because of a quarrel with his landlord, Powderly later became Grand Master Workman of the Knights of Labor, the first nationwide labor organization, after its founding in Philadelphia in 1869. By 1886 the movement had 800,000 members — an impressive number for that time. The Knights had begun as a secret 'order' whose oaths and neo-Masonic rituals were designed to protect the identity of members. Conservative Catholic churchmen objected to any such secret society, however, so Powderly agreed to revise some of the organization's practices. But it was not until James Cardinal Gibbons of Baltimore intervened with the Pope on their behalf that the Church finally decided not to condemn

CHAPTER SIX

RIGHT *South Water Street in Chicago, 1915. This street in an Irish neighborhood is crowded with horse-drawn wagons and motor trucks filled with produce for market.*

Day'. McGuire, the tenth child of Irish immigrant parents, served for many years as secretary-treasurer of the Brotherhood of Carpenters. In 1882, after he proposed a holiday to honor the workingman, 10,000 workers from the Central Labor Union marched around New York's Union Square. The celebration was such a success that it was repeated annually, until Congress made it a national holiday a dozen years later.

Many Irish-American women took jobs outside the home to support their families, and they too were active in organizing and leading the nation's fledgling labor unions. One of the most famous was Cork-born Mary Harris 'Mother' Jones, the daughter of a railroad worker, who spent much of her long life traveling cross-country, giving speeches and encouraging workers to fight for their rights. Toward the end of her career she described conditions in the southern factory where she had worked:

The lint was heavy in the room. The machinery needed constant cleaning. The tiny, slender bodies of the little children crawled in and about under dangerous machinery, oiling and cleaning. Often their hands were crushed. A finger was snapped off.

A father of two little girls worked a loom next to the one assigned to me.

"How old are the little girls?" I asked him.

"One is six years and ten days," he said, pointing to a little girl, stoop shouldered and thin chested who was threading warp, "and that one," he pointed to a pair of thin legs like twigs, sticking out from under a rack of spindles, "that one is seven and three months."

"How long do they work?"

"From six in the evening till six come morning."

"How much do they get?"

"Ten cents a night."

"And you?"

"I get forty."

Mary Harris married an iron molder in 1861 and raised four children, but they died one by one when a yellow fever epidemic swept Memphis in 1867. "The rich and the well-to-do fled the city,"

CHAPTER SIX

LEFT *The maze of
livestock pens and
walkways at Chicago's
stockyards around
1947. Many Irish
found work here.
Some, like Patrick
Cudahy, became major
figures in the meat-
packing industry.*

BELOW LEFT *"The Eighth
Wonder of the World",
the Brooklyn Bridge,
was built with Irish
labor from 1869 to
1883. This view of
pedestrians on the
upper deck promenade
of the bridge was taken
in 1910.*

FAR LEFT *A New York
City fire wagon races
to the scene of the
Triangle Shirt Factory
fire in 1911, in which
145 women, most of
them immigrants, died.
Local fire companies
were largely Irish from
the 1840s on. In 1911,
firemen of Irish descent
received 18 of the 22
medals for valor
presented to the New
York Fire department.
Another Irish-
American, future state
governor Al Smith,
was vice-chairman of
the state commission
that investigated the
fire.*

she wrote later. "The poor could not afford nurses
. . . The dead surrounded us." After her husband
also caught the fever and died, she worked for the
wealthy of Chicago as a dressmaker, where she
"had ample opportunity to observe the luxury and
extravagance of their lives". "Often I would . . .
see the poor, shivering wretches, jobless and hun-
gry, walking along the frozen lake front . . . My
employers seemed neither to notice or care . . ."

Mother Jones began attending the meetings of
the Knights of Labor and soon became an active
member. After losing her few possessions in the
Chicago Fire in 1871 she became a speaker for the
Knights, helped organize the International Workers of the World in 1905 and spent most of her
later years working for the United Mine Workers;
at 93 she traveled to West Virginia to support
striking miners there.

Elizabeth Gurley Flynn, whose grandmother
was from Galway, was also active in the IWW and
later helped found the American Communist
Party. She maintained that "an understanding of
British imperialism . . . was an open window to
all imperialism". Mary Kenney O'Sullivan, the
daughter of immigrants, was the first woman
organizer of the American Federation of Labor.
Leonora O'Reilly, who went to work in a collar
factory at age 11, joined the Knights of Labor
with her Irish-born widowed mother before becoming an organizer for the United Garment
Workers and serving on the board of the National
Women's Trade Union League.

The American Irish shared a unique combination of traits that enabled them to take the lead
in unionizing American labor. They expressed
themselves fluently and even eloquently in English, and they had a long history of negotiating
with those in power and then organizing to resist
them when necessary. But perhaps the most important quality they brought to the struggle was
an enduring loyalty to their own community and
a sense of group identity that gave them the
strength to win — ultimately — a better life for
all the nation's workers.

These same qualities also helped the American
Irish build another institution of vital importance
to the immigrant community — the Catholic
Church. The priesthood was the favored profession

CHAPTER SIX

RIGHT *New York City could be called the city the Irish built. Many of the city's most notable features — the Brooklyn Bridge, the Empire State Building, the Sixth Avenue El shown here — were built by Irish workers.*

BELOW RIGHT *The tallest building in the world when it was opened in 1931, the Empire State Building was built largely by Irish workmen. This photo of a steelworker bolting together part of the framework of the building was taken by Lewis Hine in 1930.*

for a majority of second-generation sons, and many missionary priests were sent directly from Ireland to new parishes. By the 1880s, Irish churchmen had dominated the hierarchy for over four decades, and in 1875, the choice of Irish-American John McCloskey to be the first American cardinal was proof of their unchallenged leadership. Ten years later, 35 of the 69 bishops in the United States were Irish, followed by Germans with 15, the French with 11 and the English with five. (The Dutch, Scots and Spanish all had one each.)

The completion in 1879 of the new and imposing St. Patrick's Cathedral on fashionable Fifth Avenue in New York City further symbolized the growing physical strength, prosperity and self-confidence of the Church. Between 1880 and 1920 membership nearly tripled, from 6.1 million to 17.7 million, and parochial school enrolment rose even faster, from 400,000 to 1.7 million pupils. The number of school buildings more than doubled, Catholic nursing orders established hundreds of hospitals, and thousands of cathedrals, churches, rectories, convents and seminaries went up as well. The official Catholic University, in Washington, D.C., was completed in 1889. Access to Catholic higher education helped many children of Irish-American families to earn diplomas or degrees, find better jobs, and increasingly, to enter the professions.

Scholars have called the building of the Church the most important achievement of the Irish in America. Bishop John Lancaster Spalding of Illinois insisted that, "No other people could have done for the Catholic faith in the United States what the Irish people have done," and he praised their "unalterable attachment to their priests, their deep Catholic instincts ... the unworldly

and spiritual temper of the nationaal character, their indifference to ridicule and contempt, and their unfailing generosity." By the 1880s, however, growing pressures within American society forced the hierarchy to shift its focus from building the Church physically to hammering out its position on a number of social and internal issues. Catholics were moving into the mainstream of American life and entering politics, reform movements and fraternal organizations. Congregations from other ethnic backgrounds were demanding greater recognition and representation. New nativist sympathizers, further alarmed by the depression of 1893, would soon form the American Protective Association and vow not to work with, employ or vote for Irish Catholics. How should the Church relate to all of them, and to the increasingly hostile camps of business and labor, to the Protestant-dominated society, and to the democratic process as a whole?

The leading Irish-American churchmen of the

period, whose task it was to resolve these questions, were almost all the sons of immigrants and came from working-class homes. Despite these similarities, however, they soon split into three distinct factions: a small group of radicals, based chiefly in New York City; the liberals of 'Americanists', led by Archbishop John Ireland of St. Paul and James Cardinal Gibbons of Baltimore; and the conservatives, led by John Cardinal McCloskey and his successor, Archbishop Michael Corrigan of New York, Bishop Bernard McQuaid of Rochester, and later William Cardinal O'Connel of Boston. The radicals rallied behind New York pastor Dr. Edward McGlynn, a powerful orator, a supporter of social justice and the rights of organized labor against laissez-faire capitalism, and the idol of many Irish working-class Catholics. Archbishop Corrigan and his conservatives were the complete antithesis of the progressive, egalitarian McGlynn. Rather than advocating Church-led, confrontational social change and cooperation with Protestants who espoused similar goals, they clung to an almost medieval vision of churchly order, tradition and authority. They had an abiding fear of both socialism and ecumenism, and although they condemned materialistic American values, they nonetheless defended the rights of private property and preached resignation and the spiritual value of poverty.

The New York mayoral race of 1886 became a battleground for these two opposing camps. McGlynn defied his archbishop by backing pro-labor, anti-Tammany candidate Henry George, founder of the Workingmen's Party and author of *Poverty and Progress* and the 'single-tax plan'. The Saturday night before the election, George's supporters marched 30,000 strong in a pouring rain through Union Square. Tammany made certain that the reformer lost, however, and Archbishop Corrigan suspended and then excommunicated McGlynn and exiled many of his followers to distant parishes. A papal decision later declared the priest's position compatible with Catholic social teaching and ordered him reinstated, but his career in the Church was destroyed and a clear anti-radical precedent set.

Gibbons and Ireland and their midwestern liberal allies were pragmatic moderates. While opposing trusts and political corruption, they supported the American values of democracy and individualism, emphasized the value of public schools in creating greater understanding, and wanted the Church to assist Catholics in assimilating to mainstream American culture. Gibbons especially feared that an anti-labor position would alienate Catholic workers, and strove tirelessly to prevent the Church from officially denouncing unions. "We must prove that we are the friends of the working classes," he wrote. "If we condemn or use them harshly we lose them, and they will look upon us with as much hatred and suspicion as they do in the Church of France. They commit excesses now and then. Let us correct them, but they have also real grievances. Let us help them to redress them. I would regard the condemnation of the Knights of Labor as a signal calamity to the Catholic Church of America".

The liberals triumphed in that controversy thanks chiefly to Cardinal Gibbons's tact, diplomacy and policy of 'masterly inactivity', alternating with energetic lobbying when it seemed appropriate. The paper encyclical *Rerum novarum* was issued in 1891 and ratified the progressives' position on the relationship between labor and capital.

They were less successful in winning over the Vatican on the subject of Americanization. The question had first been raised by Orestes Brownson, a New England intellectual and convert to Catholicism, who felt that the Church could not become properly American as long as it was under Irish control. Soon Germans, Italians and Poles had joined the debate, demanding more parish priests who spoke their language. Gibbons, Spalding and other 'Americanizers', however, recommended eliminating foreign customs and practices among the membership and joining with other Americans, including Protestants, in mutually beneficial social reforms. Ever the statesman, Gibbons wrote his classic *Faith of Our Fathers* as an explanation of the Catholic religion, but declared characteristically that what most gratified him about the book was that "there is

CHAPTER SIX

LEFT *Hibernian residents of Nashville, Tennessee, parade on Irish-American Day, 1897. The sociable Irish welcomed such opportunities to join their neighbors in publicly celebrating their heritage.*

RIGHT *Mary Harris Jones — known as Mother Jones — was born in Cork in 1830 and came to America at age 10. A poor widow with 6 children by 1867, she became an active worker for the Knights of Labor and later the United Mine Workers. She fought for labor reform until her death at age 100 in 1930.*

not one word in it that can give offense to our Protestant brethren."

The Pope rejected a proposal by German-Americans that the Church be reorganized along ethnic lines, but after a resurgence of nativism discredited the liberals' attempts at accommodation, he sided with the conservative majority and condemned Americanization in 1899. Only Cardinal Gibbons' efforts kept the condemnation from turning into a declaration of heresy, and the victorious conservatives set the direction for Church policy well into the twentieth century.

Gibbons and Ireland, his ally in these ideological struggles, were very different in both temperament and tactics. Ireland, born in County Kilkenny and raised in St. Paul, was a child of the frontier, an ex-Civil War chaplain and an outspoken, aggressive reformer. Gibbons was probably the most respected and distinguished of all churchmen. The son of Irish immigrants whose father died of fever during the Famine after the family had returned to Ireland, he was ordained in 1861. Seven years later, at 34, he became the 'boy bishop' of North Carolina, the youngest Catholic prelate in the world. By 1886 he was the nation's second cardinal. Below medium height and very thin, Gibbons was as discreet and conciliatory as Ireland was blunt and combative. Tolerant, benevolent and patient, he was gifted with a calm reasonableness and sensitivity to the broad movements of history that enabled him to lead the Church in an era of rapid growth and social change. The battles he and Ireland fought together to shape a more progressive American Church did not all end in decisive victories. But they moved the debate forward to a much more favorable vantage point, defined its terms and opened up new possibilities for the future.

The ferment in American society that sparked these ecclesiastical conflicts was most evident in the big cities, where the Irish and other immigrant workers were concentrated. As more and more of them arrived, settled in, and transformed their neighborhoods into ethnic enclaves, the established aristocracy who had formerly governed the cities retreated in confusion and dismay. The large numbers of Famine immigrants had created a potentially strong power base, however, and once again the Irish talent for organizing and influencing people emerged to devise new structures and new strategies to fill the vacuum.

The result was big-city machine politics. Irishmen had dominated New York City's Tammany Hall Democratic organization since the days of Mike Walsh, but by the 1870s they were in full control, and their power grew as the cities expanded. During the last decades of the century, first Brooklyn and then Boston, Chicago, Milwaukee, Jersey City, Buffalo, St. Louis and San Francisco elected Irish candidates to key positions in city government as Irish-dominated machines swung into gear.

The Irish were natural politicians — warm, witty and gregarious, flexible and practical, energetic and aggressive. To the American political scene they brought the advantages of numbers and strong clan loyalties, fluency in the language and an understanding of the Anglo-Saxon constitutional tradition. Central to their success in politics, however, was their willingness to meet the basic needs of the city's rank and file, which were ignored by Whig politicians, who believed "the best government is the one which governs least." While these entrepreneurs and businessmen argued that the interests of owners and workers were one and the same, the big-city machine 'boss' saw to it that his block and precinct captains delivered coal and groceries to the families

CHAPTER SIX

LEFT *Allan Pinkerton (smoking a pipe) with his men in Virginia, 1862. Pinkerton was chief of General McClennan's secret service. His detective agency was responsible for gathering the evidence that broke up the Molly Maguires in the 1870s.*

of laborers injured on jobs that provided no disability insurance, and paid the rent until they could go back to work. They also distributed prized patronage jobs to the unemployed, intervened at city hall for those confused by the complexities of government, aided supporters in their legal battles with landlords and the police, and sponsored parades and outings that added a touch of color to the lives of working-class families.

In effect the machines functioned as paternalistic shadow governments, and in shaping them the Irish adapted the system of neighborly loyalties and reciprocal obligations that had governed traditional village life. They also adapted the hierarchical structure that ordered their Church: at the top was the 'Boss' and below him were the ward bosses, then the precinct captains and finally the block captains. There were party clubhouses in every neighborhood — often in the local saloon — and party committees at all levels. New immigrants were frequently naturalized en masse by machine judges with few questions asked, to further expand the voting base.

The machine exacted contributions from its officeholders and candidates as well as from saloons, gambling establishments, contractors and often from organized crime. In return it guaranteed office-seekers its backing on election day, and businesses its protection and patronage throughout the year. Workingmen were asked only for their vote, which most considered a small favor to trade for the help they received year-round.

While caring for their own, however, machine politicians generally managed to enrich themselves as well at the city's expense. Politics was one of the few careers open to bright young Irish boys, who were still excluded from many Yankee banks and businesses and often could not afford to study for a profession. And like any other career it was expected to provide a good income, prestige and security. Payroll padding, overspending on public works projects and other forms of graft assured a steady flow of income to the pockets of the elect. George Washington Plunkitt had been a Tammany politician for 45 years when he was

CHAPTER SIX

CHAPTER SIX

RIGHT ABOVE *The founders of the Knights of Labor in 1865. From left to right are William Cook, James S. Wright, R.C. Macauby, James M. Hilsee, Robert W. Keen and Joseph S. Kennedy. The portrait in the center is of U.S. Stephens.*

RIGHT BELOW *Cardinal John McCloskey, the first American cardinal. The son of a Brooklyn milkman, McCloskey was deeply honored by Irish Americans, who took great pride in his accomplishment.*

interviewed in 1905, and he offered this defense against so-called machine 'corruption':

> *Everybody is talkin' these days about Tammany men growin' rich on graft, but nobody thinks of drawin' the distinction between honest graft and dishonest graft. There's all the difference in the world between the two . . . I've made a big fortune out of the game, and I'm gettin' richer every day, but I've not gone in for dishonest graft — blackmailin' gamblers, saloonkeepers, disorderly people, etc. — and neither had any of the men who have made big fortunes in politics.*
>
> *There's an honest graft, and I'm an example of how it works. I might sum up the whole thing by sayin': I seen my opportunities and I took 'em.*
>
> *Just let me explain by examples. My party's in power in the city, and it's goin' to undertake a lot of public improvements. Well, I'm tipped off, say, that they're going to lay out a new park at a certain place.*

I see my opportunity and I take it. I go to that place and I buy up all the land I can in the neighborhood. Then the board of this or that makes it plans public, and there is a rush to get my land, which nobody cared particular for before.

Ain't it perfectly honest to charge a good price and make a profit on my investment and foresight? Of course, it is. Well, that's honest graft.

Even those who might not agree with Plunkitt were often willing to overlook such practices because they created jobs for Irish suppliers, contractors and laborers, and thus acted as a crude means of redistributing the wealth.

Among the most famous practitioners of machine graft, honest or not, was William Marcy 'Boss' Tweed, a Tammany chief who ruled New York City from 1865 to 1871. Of Scotch-Irish ancestry, he had grown up as the member of an Irish street gang; his closest political associates were Peter Sweeny and Richard 'Slippery Dick' Connolly, the city comptroller. Together with Mayor Oakey Hall they made up the notorious 'Tweed Ring', which packed the courts, controlled the board of aldermen and plundered the city treasury of at least $30 million while city services deteriorated. Finally, an employee in the comptroller's office leaked information on the ring's dealings to *The New York Times*, Connolly in-

formed on the others and Tweed was indicted on 120 counts ranging from grand larceny to conspiracy. The chief prosecutor in the case was Charles O'Conor, the son of an Irish exile of '98. Connolly and Sweeny escaped to Europe with several of their stolen millions, but Tweed died in jail a few years later.

After the Tweed debacle it was 'Honest John' Kelly, the first Irish Catholic boss, who molded Tammany into a modern political organization. The complex party apparatus he created became the working model for big-city, one-party politics throughout the United States. It is often said of Kelly that he "found Tammany a horde and left it an army." A former congressman and the brother-in-law of Cardinal McCloskey, he was the son of poor immigrants from County Tyrone. John was eight when his father died, and three years later he was hired as office boy for the New York *Herald*. He was a tradesman, pugilist, volunteer fireman and saloon owner before entering politics.

Kelly eliminated any vestiges of the Tweed group from Tammany and began collecting an annual percentage of officer's salaries to create a common campaign fund. He backed business rather than labor on economic issues, however, and sponsored the election of a number of prominent businessmen to the mayor's office. Among them was William R. Grace, the city's first Irish Catholic mayor, who was elected in 1880. Born in Queenstown, County Cork, Grace had made a for-

CHAPTER SIX

BELOW LEFT
Archbishop Bayley of Baltimore imposes the Cardinal's biretta on Archbishop John McCloskey of New York at old St. Patrick's Cathedral on April 27, 1875.

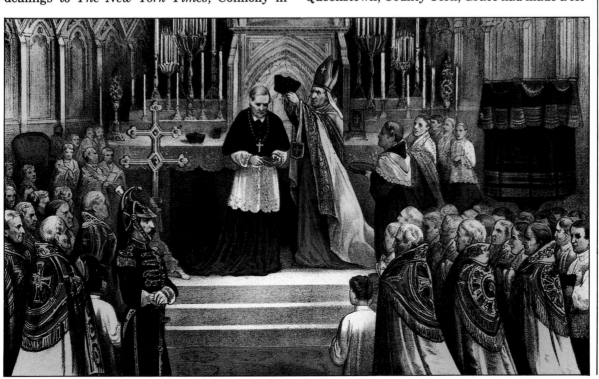

CHAPTER SIX

RIGHT ABOVE *The famous bronze doors of St. Patrick's Cathedral in New York City. They welcome visitors to the largest Roman Catholic cathedral in America.*

RIGHT BELOW *The original "St. Pat's" is old St. Patrick's church on Mulberry Street in lower Manhattan, New York City. The area had a strong Irish population throughout the 1800s.*

tune selling supplies for transoceanic shipping before starting his own steamship line. He later gained control over Peruvian silver mines and other invaluable resources in exchange for refinancing that country's national debt. He served two terms in City Hall and was an able, efficient administrator.

During the 1870s and 1880s depression had been followed by recession, mass unemployment and social unrest. Mary Elizabeth Lease, the 'Queen of the Populists', whose Irish father was killed fighting for the Union during the Civil War, was one of many agitators who spoke out against big business and big government during the last decades of the century. In the mayoral election of 1886, Tammany nontheless adhered to the pro-business course set by Kelly and supported millionaire businessman Abram Hewitt against the radical reformer Henry George. Many suspected fraud when Hewitt won. The man who engineered the victory was Richard Croker, who had inherited the mantle of leadership from Kelly just months before he died.

Croker's father brought his large family to New York from County Cork in 1846, when Richard was three. They lived first in an Irish shantytown where Central Park now stands, but later moved to better housing on East Twenty-Eighth Street. Although Richard attended grade school, he remained as uneducated as he was shrewd and ruthless. He too had been a fireman and prizefighter and worked as a railroad machinist for a while, but at 25 Tammany awarded him a seat on the board of aldermen for his services as captain of a gang of election repeaters. Six years later Croker was indicted for shooting a man in an election dispute but was never convicted, and after a number of minor jobs he won back his old seat on the board of aldermen before becoming Tammany's Chief Sacham.

Croker extended and standardized the system of machine politics that Kelly had introduced and during the next 10 years amassed a fortune of over $8 million, largely from inside business ventures. He excluded the wealthy conservatives Kelly had cultivated. During his tenure Tammany welcomed many young Jewish politicians into the party and accorded the new immigrants power and representation in Congress. Although he ran New York as a wide-open town until Protestant clergymen began an anti-vice crusade, a subsequent reform administration was short-lived and in the end it was the great 'Ice Trust' scandal of 1900 that drove him from power. When an investigating committee learned that the

CHAPTER SIX

LEFT ABOVE *Celebrating the 100th year of St. Patrick's Cathedral in 1979. Construction on the Cathedral began in 1858 and was completed in 1879. The Lady Chapel behind the high altar was added later.*

city's leading politicians had received shares in a new ice monopoly in exchange for granting exclusive rights to unload the ice at municipal docks, enraged citizens voted with their pocketbooks and elected a new reform coalition. Croker retired to his Irish estate, saw his racehorse Orby win the English Derby in 1907, and died in bed 15 years later, leaving an estate of $5 million.

One of the dock commissioners involved in the Ice Trust was Charles Francis Murphy, who rose to the leadership of Tammany in 1903 and held sway for the next 20 years. A taciturn conservative, Murphy waged a long-running battle with erstwhile reformer William Randolph Hearst until the publisher accepted Murphy's offer to have him nominated for governor in 1906. After betraying his principles, however, Hearst lost the election and three years later was defeated for mayor of New York by William Jay Gaynor, the son of an Irish immigrant farmer. Colorful, cantankerous and honest, Gaynor nevertheless was too ouspoken to earn Tammany's renomination, and he died while running for reelection as an independent in 1913.

Another picturesque character of the period was 'Big Tim' Sullivan, the son of an Irish laborer on New York's Lower East Side. Tim went to work for Tammany at 15 and was eventually elected to the state legislature and to Congress. Although he ran a vice empire and collected his share of graft, he also dispensed food and clothes to the poor and was a generous supporter of liberal causes, including women's suffrage, out of gratitude to a teacher who had bought him a pair of shoes when he was a slum child. Tim was given the job of organizing the Bowery for Tammany beginning in 1890, when Italian and Jewish immigrants were replacing the Irish there. He and other machine stalwarts strove to bring these new voters into the fold by distributing free coal and ice, taking them on outings, intervening for them in court and attending their social gatherings; Tim even got the state legislature to declare Columbus Day a legal holiday to please his Italian constituents. The strategy worked, and it produced an ethnic coalition of Jewish, Italian and Irish voters that assured Tammany's hegemony for decades to come. When Tim was struck by a train and killed in 1913, his funeral drew 25,000 mourners, another testament to the appeal of his — and Tammany's — personal approach to politics.

By the 1890s the Irish-American style in politics was winning top offices in cities across the country. Thomas Taggart, from County Monaghan, gained the mayor's chair in Indianapolis

CHAPTER SIX

RIGHT *Cardinal Spellman Hall at Fordham University, New York City. Known equally for academic excellence and high-level athletics, Fordham is the alma mater for several generations of Irish Catholics.*

LEFT BELOW *Political and social life often went hand-in-hand for the Irish. This fancy-dress ball took place at Tammany Hall on November 15, 1906 as a political fundraiser. Note the bagpiper all the way to the right in the top row.*

in 1895 and went on to serve as chairman of the Democratic National Committee from 1904 to 1916 and as United States senator from Indiana. Irish-Americans Edward F. Dunne and William E. Dever led reform administrations in Chicago, and Thomas A. Burke managed to mediate among the interests of Cleveland's more than 50 nationality groups during his four terms as mayor. He was later elected to the United States Senate.

Despite their cultural and economic exclusion by the old-line Yankee establishment the Irish had been a force in Boston politics for years, and in 1886 they elected Hugh O'Brien as the city's first Irish Catholic mayor. Born in County Fermanagh, O'Brien had come to Boston as a child and rose from printer's apprentice to become publisher of a major newspaper there. Patrick Collins, former Fenian, Irish-American leader and reform mayor from 1902 to 1905, was just an infant when he was brought from Ireland by his widowed mother during the Famine. He worked as an upholsterer and a coal miner before putting himself through Harvard Law School, and becoming a wealthy businessman. Collins also served as Democratic National Committee chairman and

LEFT *The family of James Cardinal Gibbons came to America in 1829. Young James was ordained in 1861 and became Cardinal in 1886. He was one of the ablest of many Irish-American prelates. This photo was taken in 1891.*

as President Cleveland's Consul General in London. John F. 'Honey Fitz' Fitzgerald, grandfather of the late President, was a political boss in Boston before winning the mayoralty in 1905 and again in 1909. It was during his tenure that the Irish finally wrested political control of the city from the Yankee aristocracy. One of nine sons of a neighborhood grocer, Fitzgerald was a friendly, lively man whose nickname was a reference to his pleasant tenor voice; his rendition of 'Sweet Adeline' became a trademark of all his campaigns.

The man who succeeded Fitzgerald as mayor of Boston, James Michael Curley, had a career that spanned almost half a century and set the style for a whole generation of young politicians. His parents emigrated from Galway as adolescents and settled in a slum neighborhood of Boston, where their two sons were born. After his father died Curley's mother worked as a scrubwoman to support him and his brother. Young James sold papers and delivered groceries, carrying bushels of flour up rickety tenement steps, but in 1899 he launched his political career by winning a seat on the City Council. By the time he became mayor in 1913 he had already served two terms in Congress.

CHAPTER SIX

RIGHT *Tammany hall in 1812, at the corner of Frankfort and Nassau Streets in New York City. A few decades later, the Tammany political machine had outgrown the building and moved.*

RIGHT BELOW *Head of the notorious "Tweed Ring", William Marcy Tweed (1823–1878) controlled the politics of New York City through Tammany Hall from 1857 almost until his death. With his cronies, "Boss" Tweed is thought to have defrauded the city of at least $30 million. Reformers such as Thomas Nast led to his downfall; Tweed died penniless in prison. He is shown here in the uniform of a volunteer fireman.*

Before his final defeat for the same office 36 years later Curley would serve three more terms as mayor, one in Congress and one as governor of Massachusetts. A tall, muscular man with a slashing wit and a carefully cultivated baritone voice, he was defeated as often as he was elected in the course of an up-and-down history. Observers have praised him as an able and energetic executive who built medical and recreational facilities and provided jobs in a city afflicted with chronic unemployment. But above all Curley was a showman and fighter who used his talent for invective to aggressively attack the 'reactionary' Yankee establishment. As a spokesman for Boston's Irish-Americans he dramatized the resentment they felt toward those who labeled them second-class citizens, and in so doing he built a long and successful political career. But by exploiting those animosities he also prolonged the destructive divisions within the city and prevented the solution of many pressing social and economic problems whose causes were more complex than Yankee dominance.

The presidential election of 1884 demonstrated that the Irish were a force to be reckoned with in national politics as well. The Republican candidate was Secretary of State James G. Blaine and the Democrats nominated New York Governor Grover Cleveland. Both parties wooed the Empire State's half-million Irish voters. Blaine's campaign emphasized his strong anti-British record and that his mother was a Catholic; his cousin, Sister Angela (who became his 'sister' as election day grew closer), was described as the mother superior of a convent. Patrick Ford, the influential editor of *Irish World,* came out in support of Blaine. New York's *Irish American,* meanwhile, emphasized that Cleveland's mother had been Miss O'Neill before she married, and reminded readers of the Republican's party's "unvarying anti-Irish proclivities . . ." Democrats also attacked Blaine as a prohibitionist and Know-Nothing.

On the eve of the election, however, Blaine's supporters were optimistic. Both parties knew the race was a close one, but Irish voters were coming around to the Republican side and no less an authoritative source than a Tammany leader had warned the Democratic nominating convention that "Cleveland cannot carry the state of New York". Then, just days before the election, a Presbyterian clergyman named Samuel D. Burchard, speaking for his delegation of Protestant ministers, assured Blaine that, "We are your friends, Mr. Blaine, and . . . We expect to vote for you next Tuesday . . . We are Republicans, and don't pro-

LEFT *The powerful political caricatures of Thomas Nast (1840–1902) helped bring down mighty Boss Tweed. In this drawing from 1895, Nast caricatures himself in the center and Tweed above left and right.*

pose to ... identify ourselves with the party whose antecedents have been *rum, Romanism and rebellion.*"

The following Sunday Democrats distributed handbills publicizing the remark to Catholic churches throughout the country, and Blaine further damaged his standing with working-class Irish by allowing wealthy Republic supporters to sponsor a fancy dinner for him at Delmonico's. On election night Cleveland carried the state by less than 1,200 votes out of 1.76 million cast, and became the first Democratic president since 1861. Four years later he was forced by Irish leaders to expel British Amabassador Sir Lionel Sackville-West after the ambassador was tricked into advising a correspondent to vote for Cleveland because he could be counted on to defend British interests. President McKinley officially acknowledged the nation's growing Irish-American political presence when he appointed Joseph McKenna to be Attorney General in 1897 — the first Irish-American Catholic to hold a Cabinet post. McKenna later served as an Associate Justice of the Supreme Court from 1898 to 1925. Maurice F. Egan, an Irish-American writer and educator, was named Minister to Denmark by Theodore Roosevelt in 1907; in 1916 he arranged the U.S. purchase of the Danish West Indies, now the Virgin Islands.

The American Irish had definitely made their mark as citizens and as voters, and the political structures they had built so painstakingly had served them well; by 1920, there were more than twice as many Irish members of Congress as all other foreign-born members combined. These intricate and carefully ordered party organizations reflected the background and values of the men who created them: pragmatic, patriarchal, communal rather than individualistic. The machines emphasized bread-and-butter issues rather than ideology and provided a buffer between working-class families and the harsh realities of laissez-faire capitalism. But their primary purpose was winning power and then keeping it, and they tolerated and even encouraged corruption and graft, subservience and hypocrisy. By introducing many immigrants to the American political system, and by teaching them to work together, they helped an increasingly diverse democratic society to succeed. But a more sophisticated electorate eventually demanded more broadly based social programs at the state and national level to replace the old personal approach to social problems, and the era of the big-city machine politician drew to a close.

The success of the Irish as labor leaders, churchmen and politicians also extended to other areas of national life. In two or three generations and often in just one, thousands of Irish-Americans achieved national recognition in business, social service, sports and the arts. Their contributions helped shape the evolving landscape and culture of the country at a crucial time in its history.

CHAPTER SIX

RIGHT AND OPPOSITE
RIGHT *"Evolution of
the Murphy." This
satirical, anti-Irish
cartoon depicting the
rise of an Irish
immigrant from
bewildered new arrival
to policeman to
political leader
appeared in* Judge *in
1891.*

RIGHT CENTER *The title
of this 1887 woodcut
cartoon from* Leslie's
Magazine *is "Election
Day scene at close of
polls — Tammany Hall
in danger." Local
district leaders often
set up booths near the
polls and manipulated
the vote.*

EVOLUTION OF THE MURPHY.

THE COCOON.

THE GOSSOON.

THE MULDOON.

Many successful Irish-American businessmen
have built — literally — the nation's cities. John
B. McDonald came to New York in 1847 and got
his first job in construction with the aid of his
contractor father's Tammany connections. He
went on to build a New York City subway as well
as portions of the Illinois Central and Baltimore
and Ohio rail lines. Another son of an Irish contractor, Daniel Crimmins, erected more than 400
buildings and laid miles of streets and gas lines as
well as much of New York's elevated tracks.
Thomas Fortune Ryan, who gained control of the
city's transportation lines in 1900, headed a vast
financial empire than included interests in banking, insurance, railroads, tobacco and African
mines and rubber plantations. William Wilson
Corcoran, born in Baltimore to Irish parents, became a successful banker, broker and philan-
thropist in Washington and built the Corcoran
Gallery of Art there.

Other enterprising Irish-Americans have
worked to develop the nation's mineral resources.
James McClurg Guffey, whose Scotch-Irish parents lived in Pennsylvania, was the first to drill

BEGINNING TO BLOSSOM.

THE ALDERMAN.

THE GRAND SACHEM—FULL OF HONORS.

for oil and gas in many parts of Kansas, Texas, California, West Virginia and Indian Territory. Wisconsin-born Edward L. Doheny, son of an Irish Famine immigrant, ran away from home at age 16 and became a gold prospector before making millions in California and Mexican oil; he was later one of the principals in the famous Teapot Dome oil scandal.

Irish imagination and ingenuity also produced a number of inventions around the turn of the century that quickly became household words. In 1888 John Robert Gregg devised the Gregg system of shorthand, now the most widely used transcription system worldwide, and brought it to the United States when he emigrated five years later. The space-saving Murphy bed that so often folded up into a wall and trapped the Little Tramp during his cinematic adventures was the creation of William Lawrence Murphy, the son of Irish immigrants who traveled to Tuolumne City, California, during the Gold Rush. Henry Ford, the man whose assembly-line production techniques made the motor car affordable to the average workingman, was the grandson of a Famine

RIGHT ABOVE *William Russell Grace came to America from Cork as a cabin boy in the 1840s. He made his fortune in steamship lines. The early headquarters of W.R. Grace & Co., founded in 1865, were in this building on Hanover Square in New York City. Grace was elected Mayor of the city in 1880 and again in 1884.*

RIGHT BELOW *John F. Fitzgerald, maternal grandfather of President John Fitzgerald Kennedy, was mayor of Boston in 1906.*

immigrant from County Cork. His Ford Motor Company, established in 1903, marketed its first Model T in 1908 for $850 dollars and its last one in 1925 for a sticker price of $260; by 1928 it had sold over 15,000,000 cars and is today the world's largest auto manufacturer.

Michael Cudahy and William Kelly were two more Irish-Americans whose creativity transformed their respective industries. Cudahy's parents brought their children to America from Kilkenny during the Famine and the boy left school at 14 to work in a meat-packing firm. After being promoted to a partnership in Armour and Company and supervising their Chicago stockyard operations, he completely changed established production and distribution patterns as well as the nation's eating habits by introducing refrigerated processing and transportation of the company's meat products. The Cudahy Packing Company, which he started with his brothers John and Patrick, made all of them fortunes. William Kelly, the son of an Irish immigrant who settled in Pittsburgh, established that city as the center of a new industry when he developed the basic process for producing steel and patented the converter that was its key figure. Another immigrant's son, James Augustine Farrell, took a job in a steel factory in 1879 when he was age 16 and eventually rose to the presidency of the U.S. Steel Corporation, a position he held from 1911 to 1932.

Burns International Security Services, which provides guards to business and industry, is named for William J. Burns, the son of Irish-Americans from Baltimore, who gained fame as a master detective in the days before electronic surveillance. He opened the Burns Detective Agency in 1900 before becoming a Secret Service agent and director of the Federal Bureau of Investigation, a post he held from 1924 to 1924. Another noted Irish-American public servant was W J McGee, the son of an immigrant miner, who learned to write with the help of his schoolteacher wife and always insisted on the right to use his initials without periods. A respected anthropologist, geographer and conservationist, McGee also served as secretary of the National Conservation Commission. Thomas Henry Barry, a striking example of the Irish warrior tradition, was a New Yorker who graduated from West Pont and joined the predominantly Irish 7th Cavalry soon after its catastrophic defeat at the Little Bighorn. He served on the frontier, in the Spanish-American War, in the Philippines and in China during the Boxer Rebellion before being appointed superintendent of the U.S. Military

LEFT *William Cullen Bryant (1794–1878) was a poet and also the editor of the New York City Evening Post from 1826 to his death. He advocated free trade, abolitionism and many other reforms.*

Academy in 1910 and then commanding general of the army's Central Department after the outbreak of World War I. Maria McCreery, a prominent fighter for women's rights and member of the Wisconsin Woman Suffrage Association, was the granddaughter of Irish immigrants. Margaret Sanger took a different and highly controversial approach to improving the situation of women when she launched her campaign to make standard methods of birth control available to poor families. Her own Irish mother had borne 11 children and died at an early age. Margaret worked as a maternity nurse among tenement dwellers on Manhattan's Lower East Side before challenging the Comstock Act, which labeled contraceptive information obscene, and opening her own clinic in Brooklyn in 1916. She eventually won her case before the U.S. Court of Appeals.

Their physical strength and competitive instinct led many poor Irish boys to seek fame and fortune as prizefighters, a sport they dominated during the second half of the nineteenth century, when boxing and gambling were still illegal. John 'Old Smoke' Morrissey, who traveled from Tipperary to New York as a child, became a factory hand at 12 and learned to fight as a saloon bouncer and boardinghouse runner. A great 'broth of a bhoy', Morrissey was 22 in 1853 when he won the American heavyweight championship from Yankee Sullivan in a 37-round bare-knuckles bout. He earned his nickname in a legendary barroom brawl when he knocked over a stove and fell backward on the coals, but still got up and delivered a blow that downed his adversary. Morrissey later opened the nation's first fashionable gambling house at Saratoga Springs and was elected to the state legislature and twice to Congress. When he died in 1878, the governor, dozens of legislators and 15,000 workingmen and women came to pay their respects to the 'Poor Boy of Tipperary'.

The great John L. Sullivan gave the sport of boxing its modern form when he adopted the Marquis of Queensberry rules, but only after defeating Paddy Ryan for the heavyweight title in 1882 and vanquishing challenger Jake Kilrain in a bloody 75-round battle seven years later. The son of an immigrant hod carrier, Sullivan was a popular hero who toured the United States and the British Isles and was celebrated for his boast that he could "lick any sonofabitch alive"! After years of high living, however, he lost his title in 1892 to another Irish-American, 'Gentleman Jim' Corbett. Irish fans never forgave the San Franciscan for defeating their beloved 'Boston Strong

Boy', but Sullivan withdrew to the stage as an actor and temperance lecturer and never fought again.

Baseball captured the imagination of America just as the Irish were taking up a larger role in national life, and Irish players and managers helped establish the game even before the Civil War. Among its many early stars were Michael J. 'King' Kelly, whose fame as a base-runner was celebrated in the song 'Slide, Kelly, Slide', and John Joseph 'Muggsy' McGraw, who played infield for the Baltimore Orioles before becoming manager of the New York Giants in 1902, when he was 29, and winning ten National League pennants. Charles A. Comiskey, the son of a Famine immigrant and Chicago ward politician, started playing third base for Milwaukee in 1875, at 17, and after a long career helped organize the American League; he also owned the Chicago White Sox until his death in 1931. Outstanding among Irish representatives of the game's 'Golden Age' and its all-time grand old man, however, was the great Connie Mack (Cornelius McGillicuddy), a brilliant catcher and later manager of the Philadelphia Athletics.

Famous Irish Olympic medalists of the period include runners Thomas Burke and Michael Sheridan, and James Connolly of South Boston, who won the triple jump. Demonstrating physical prowess of another sort, saloonkeeper Steve Brodie became an overnight celebrity in 1886 when, on a bet, he became the first man to survive a leap from the Brooklyn Bridge. Skeptics speculated that the 23-year-old Brodie actually pushed a dummy off instead, but he collected his $200 prize money nonetheless.

As the Irish and other Americans became more settled, prosperous and well-educated their interest in the arts grew as well, and the flowering of the Irish-American community produced many well-known composers, performers, journalists and other contributors to the nation's cultural life. In the fine arts, New York-born sculptor James Edward Kelly captured the dash and daring of perhaps the most famous Irish-American general with his sculpture 'Sheridan's Ride'. His many other works include busts of Civil War and Spanish-American War heroes and equestrian statues of Paul Revere and Theodore Roosevelt. Together they earned their creator the popular title 'sculptor of American history'. Thomas Hovenden was an Irish orphan who came to America during the Civil War, studied art in New York and Paris, and painted 'The Last Moments of John Brown', which hangs in the Metropolitan

LEFT BELOW *Oil magnate Edward L. Doheny (left), born in America of Irish parents, was implicated in the Teapot Dome scandal of the 1920s. Doheny was acquitted. He is shown here with attorney Frank Hogan in 1930. Hogan later became District Attorney of New York City.*

RIGHT *John Joseph McGraw (1873–1934), son of an Irish immigrant railroad worker, was the beloved manager of the New York Giants baseball club for many years. He was the first to take baseball abroad, taking exhibition teams to Cuba, South America, Japan and elsewhere. He is shown here in Cuba in 1930.*

Museum. One of the greatest American architects, Louis Henri Sullivan, was the son of a wandering Irish musician and dancing master from County Cork. He was the most influential architect at work around the turn of the century and his many skyscrapers and design for the Transportation Building at the World's Columbian Exposition made him the acknowledged 'father of modernism in architecture'. The son of an Irish mother and a French shoemaker father, Augustus Saint-Gaudens was born in Dublin and moved to Boston with his parents when he was only six months old. They later settled in New York City, where the boy was apprenticed to a cameo cutter. In 1873 he set up his studio there and launched a career that brought him worldwide fame as one of the greatest sculptors of all time.

With their love of music and poetry, native charm, quick wit and flair for drama and storytelling, the Irish were natural performers. They earned a name for themselves in the American theater as early as the 1830s, when William Grattan Tyrone Power, great-grandfather of the film star Tyrone Power and theater director Tyrone Guthrie, made several triumphant tours of American cities playing comic Irish roles. During the

middle of the nineteenth century, Dubliner Dion Boucicault wrote and acted in many plays about gallant, sensitive Irish immigrants, and Limerick-born Ada Rehan was a favorite leading lady in many Shakespearean and Restoration comedies during the 1880s and 1890s. In 1882, the accomplished Shakespearean actor James O'Neill scored such a success as Edmond Dantes in *The Count of Monte Cristo* that he never played another role as celebrated. His son, playwright Eugene O'Neill, recorded his father's bitterness at his failure to break out of the part in *A Long Day's Journey into Night*.

After studying music in Germany and Austria and marrying the prima donna of the Vienna Opera, Dublin-born Victor Herbert arrived in the United States in 1886 and was soon acknowledged as the major American composer of light opera. He also wrote music for films and for several Ziegfeld Follies, but he will always be best remembered for the romantic charm and lyrical genius of operettas such as *The Red Mill, Naughty Marietta* and *Babes in Toyland*.

In a more popular vein, Irish-American comedians such as Gallagher and Sheehan delighted vaudeville audiences, and Pat Rooney from Cork

LEFT *Tyrone Power, shown here in his swashbuckling role in* The Black Rose, *was the great-grandson of William Grattan Tyrone Power, a famed Irish actor who died in 1841. Tyrone Power (1914–1958) was the fourth generation of his family to enter the theater. Another of William's great-grandsons, Tyrone Guthrie (1900–1971), was famed as a stage director.*

CENTER *The eldest of six children born to immigrants from Kilmalooda Parish, County Cork, Henry Ford (1863–1947) was the first to make an automobile anyone could afford. He designed the Model T in 1908; by the time the model was discontinued 20 years later, over 15 million had been sold. The cost of a Model T in 1928 was $260. Ford is shown here with his first car in an undated photograph.*

was the first of three generations of Irish song-and-dance men to win American hearts; his grandson, Mickey Rooney, followed his father and grandfather into the theater. But the most brilliant luminaries to rule the New York musical theater during the 1880s and 1890s were the singer/actor/writer team of Edward Harrigan and Tony Hart. After getting their start in vaudeville, they produced a steady stream of comedies about American Irish life that featured a succession of impulsive, extroverted but short-tempered 'stage Irish' types such as the boisterous Civil War veteran Dan Mulligan of the Mulligan Guards. The songs from these shows, including 'Why Paddy's Always Poor', 'Remember, Boy, You're Irish', 'The Pitcher of Beer' and 'Give an Honest Irish Boy a Chance', became instant hits, but by the turn of the century the pair's last major success, *Reilly and the 400,* was making fun of the new rich 'lace curtain' Irish with the song 'Maggie Murphy's Home':

> There's an organ in the parlour, to give
>   the house a tone,
> And you're welcome every evening at
>   Maggie Murphy's home.

A campaign by the Ancient Order of Hibernians early in the new century hastened the demise of the stereotypic stage Irishman, and soon a new kind of Irish performer would win acclaim for his ardent American patriotism as much as for his declaration that he was:

> Proud of all the Irish blood that's in me
> Divil a man can say a word agin me.

George Michael Cohan (originally Keohane) was an outstanding entertainer whose career in the theater spanned more than 50 years. During that time he wrote, produced and performed in countless plays and musicals and made famous such perennial song favorites as 'You're a Grand Old Flag', 'Give My Regards to Broadway', and 'Harrigan'. Although he was not really "born on the Fourth of July" as he claimed in "I'm a Yankee Doodle Dandy", his patriotic father had officially moved the boy's birthdate up a day so that it coincided with the birthday of the nation. Outgoing, enthusiastic, extraordinarily talented and versatile, George M. Cohan was the ultimate Irish-American entertainer.

RIGHT *Augustus Saint-Gaudens, born in Dublin in 1848, came to America as a child. He became the foremost American sculptor of his time, best known for his public monuments. This memorial frieze in Boston commemorates Robert Shaw, who died leading black troops in an assault during the Civil War.*

RIGHT BELOW *Songs about the homeland and the experience of emigration were often included in musical shows and later sold as sheet music. The multi-talented actor and playwright Dion Boucicault also wrote the lyrics to this musical tale of Pat Malloy from Kilkenny.*

As the Irish began to participate more fully in all these different areas of American life, growing numbers of Irish-American authors and journalists were starting to reflect and comment on their community's concerns and its role in the nation's culture. Ever since Thomas O'Connor founded *The Shamrock* in New York in 1810, similar newspapers had sprung up — and often withered just as quickly for lack of funds — wherever there was a sizeable Irish community. John Boyle O'Reilly, who became proprietor and editor of the Boston *Pilot* in 1876, was one of the most talented and esteemed Irish-American journalists of his day. A Drogheda native and former Fenian who had been sentenced to death, then banished to Australia before escaping to the United States, he defended minorities and immigrants, wrote several critically acclaimed volumes of poetry, and was a spokesman for the nation's Irish as well as a respected member of the Boston literary establishment at the time of his death in 1890. Another prominent editor and ethnic leader, Patrick Ford, was brought to Boston as an orphan in 1842, started *The Irish World* in New York in 1870, and inspired a debate that sparked innovative attempts to help immigrant workers adjust to the expanding industrial system. The paper eventually absorbed its long-time rival, John Devoy's passionately anti-British *Gaelic American,* which the ex-Fenian founded in 1903 and edited until his death 25 years later. The first of a long line of Irish-American literary magazines, *The Celtic Monthly,* was published and edited by James Haltigan in New York City during the 1870s and 1880s.

Finley Peter Dunne was an Irish-American journalist and also one of the greatest satirists America has produced. His 'Mr. Dooley' sketches, which first appeared in the depression year of 1893, featured the popular dialect monologues of an Irish bachelor and saloonkeeper who served as his creator's mouthpiece for more than 20 years. Martin Dooley and his friend Hennessey were drawn as typical members of the Irish community at a time when that community, while suffering economically, was becoming increasingly self-confident and self-aware. Martin Dooley discussed all of its foibles, including those of the policeman who 'dhrinks this beat', as well as other immigrant groups, local machine politicians and corrupt businessmen. But after Dunne moved from his native Chicago to New York his columns dealt increasingly with national and international issues, and it was these pieces — skeptical, irreverent and humane — that won

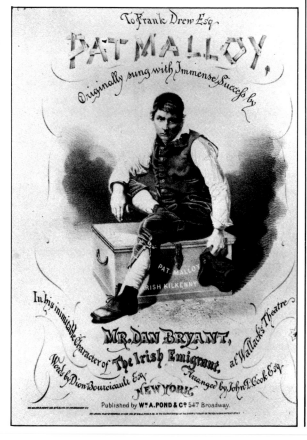

INTERNATIONAL HEAVYWEIGHT
CHAMPIONSHIP
OF THE
WORLD

Jack Dempsey vs Georges Carpentier

THIRTY ACRES OVAL   JERSEY CITY
N. J.
JULY 2, 1921
UNDER THE MANAGEMENT OF TEX RICKARD

Preliminary Bouts to
World's Heavyweight Championship

Saturday, July 2, 1921

LEFT *Boxing was one*
way an Irish boy could
make his way up. This
poster is for the famed
Dempsey-Carpentier
fight in 1921; Dempsey
won. Note the Irish
names listed among the
fighters in the
preliminary bouts.

BELOW LEFT *Katherine*
Hepburn starred as the
drug-addicted mother
in the 1962 film version
of Eugene O'Neill's
autobiographical play
Long Day's Journey
Into Night.

RIGHT *Son of the popular Irish song-and-dance man Pat Rooney, Mickey Rooney, while still unmistakably Irish, has played a wide range of stage and screen roles.*

CENTER *The theatrical partnership of Edward Harrigan and Tony Hart lasted for over 30 years, starting in the 1870s. Their good-natured comic and musical portrayals of immigrant life in general and Irish immigrant life in particular were immensely popular.*

him lasting renown. He never lost his typically Irish perspective on history, however, and the Irishman's bitter memories of British rule prompted him to rephrase two favorite slogans of the imperialist zeal that swept America after the Spanish-American War as follows: 'Hands across th' sea an' into somewan's pocket', and 'Take up th' white man's burden an' hand it to the coons'.

The work of another Irish-American humorist, George McMannus, also portrayed the Irish as a community in transition. The main characters in his comic strip 'Bringing up Father', which he created in 1913, are a former hod carrier named Jiggs who has struck it rich but is still an immigrant at heart, and his social-climbing wife Maggie. Maggie is constantly trying to drag him to the opera with their rich neighbors the Van Snoots, while Jiggs prefers to spend his evenings playing cards with the boys at Dinty's. McMannus got the idea for his strip, the first to achieve worldwide fame, when he saw a play about a newly rich Irish family called *The Rising Generation* at the St. Louis Opera House, where his immigrant father was manager. A more tragic view of the Irish-American experience is apparent in Stephen Crane's novels *Maggie: A Girl of the Streets* (1893) and *George's Mother* (1896), sociological portraits of lower-class Irish life at the turn of the century.

The entrance of the Irish into the American

PARADE.

SONG BY ED. HARRIGAN.

RAHAM
SUCCESS BY
N & HART.

RK,
nd & C.º 547 Broadway.

mainstream and their rise to prominence in so many different fields did not, however, efface the memory of their homeland and its ongoing struggle for independence. The Orange Riots of 1870 and 1871 were proof that the old loyalties — and animosities — were still strong. When close to 2,500 New York Orangemen held their first major celebration, which was to include a picnic, parade and dance, on July 12, 1870, about 200 people followed them shouting insults and were soon joined by a crowd of close to 300 Irish laborers working along the route. The picnic grounds quickly became a battleground as the workmen and those with them hurled stones and the unarmed Orangemen responded with clubs, shovels and anything else they could find. After the Irish had regrouped they returned for a second encounter. Shots were fired and police had to break up the hostilities.

The following year the Irish Hibernian Society declared that it would disrupt any attempt to repeat the Orange celebration, and when the Protestants asked for protection the superintendent of police outlawed their planned parade to forestall any violence. A deluge of complaints that they had turned over control of the city's streets to the Irish persuaded the mayor and governor to reverse that decision, however, and instead they sent a force of 700 police and 5,000 militiamen to protect fewer than 100 Orangemen. Even so, shots rang out at points along the parade route until at Eighth Avenue and Twenty-Fourth Street a single shot was fired and the militia, acting without orders, loosed a barrage that killed 37 civilians and wounded 67 others. Two members of the police and militia were also killed and 24 wounded, primarily by their own bullets. Writing in the Boston *Pilot*, John Boyle O'Reilly emphasized that although the Irish bore "the blame and

BELOW
Composer and conductor Victor Herbert was born in Ireland in 1859. He came to America in 1886 and was the conductor of the Pittsburgh Symphony Orchestra from 1898 to 1904. He is best known for his delightful operettas, particularly Babes in Toyland *(1903). Herbert died in 1924; in 1939 Allan Jones and Mary Martin starred in the film of his life,* The Great Victor Herbert.

RIGHT *The creator of the fictitious "Mr. Dooley", whose humorous comments on Irish life in America appeared from 1893 to 1913, was Finley Peter Dunne (1867–1936). He appears here, second from left, at Mark Twain's 70th birthday dinner at Delmonico's in 1905.*

the shame" for the riots, 'Irish Catholics . . . as a body, condemn all breach of the law in attacking an Orange procession, just as honestly as they would condemn a riot of any other criminal nature". He spoke for the growing numbers of Irish-Americans who found such violent behavior unacceptable.

Also in 1870, President Grant let it be known that his administration would no longer tolerate armed raids by the Fenian 'government in exile' against British territory in Canada. So when John Devoy, Jeremiah O'Donovan Rossa and the other Fenian leaders known as the 'Cuban Five' (after the *Cuba*, the ship they traveled on) landed in New York in January of 1871, they threw their support behind a new and even more radical organization. Known as the Clan na Gael, or 'children of the clan', it was a tightly knit and avowedly secret society that advocated direct military action against the British to achieve a revolution in Ireland.

Clan na Gael was founded in 1867 by Jerome H. Collins but Devoy soon dominated the organization, which attracted many other ex-Fenians as well as respected Irish-American politicians, businessmen and professionals. The Clan adopted the basic strategy devised by the Fenians in the 1850s: Irish-Americans would supply guns and money for Irish liberation movements and also mobilize public opinion against American foreign policy decisions that favored the British. This belief that "England's difficulty is Ireland's opportunity" led Clansmen to finance John Holland's efforts during the 1870s and 1880s to develop a submarine that would destroy the British navy. Holland, an Irish-American schoolmaster, named an 1881 version of his invention the *Fenian Ram,* and his later prototypes were bought and used by the U.S. Navy to build its first successful submarine.

During the mid-1870s the Clan gained popular respect for rescuing Fenian prisoners from Australia, but rural prosperity in Ireland and depression in the U.S. discouraged any other revolutionary activities. When O'Donovan Rossa became impatient and started collecting money for a 'Skirmishing Fund' to dynamite English cities many Irish-Americans were shocked, but by 1877 the fund totaled nearly $50,000.

That same year the Clan formally allied itself with the Irish Republican Brotherhood, the Irish branch of the Fenians, and the two groups organized a joint revolutionary directory to plan the coming fight for Irish independence. At the same time, a large number of Irish nationalists aban-

doned the conciliatory approach of Isaac Butt, a member of Parliament who had launched the Home Rule movement, and rallied behind another Home Rule M.P. named Charles Stewart Parnell, a young Protestant landlord from Wicklow and the grandson of Admiral Charles Stewart of Philadelphia, a distinguished American naval officer. Parnell had switched to a policy of obstruction in the House of Commons; his charismatic leadership soon made him the new messiah of Irish nationalism.

Beginning in 1877, disastrous potato harvests in Ireland had combined with a drop in farm prices and a sharp rise in the number of evictions to revive memories of the Famine. John Devoy wanted to exploit the situation politically, and together with other Irish nationalists and Clan members he formulated a plan called the New Departure: Parnell would continue to work in the Commons for Home Rule while republicans mobilized Irish peasant farmers. Parnell would demand that Parliament grant Home Rule. If it did not, he and his followers would establish an Irish Parliament in Dublin, defended by shock troops armed with American guns.

Parnell, who remained the acknowledged leader of the nationalist cause, considered the plan viable, but he did favor the idea of land reform. In 1879 Michael Davitt, 'the Father of the Land League', began mobilizing 8,000,000 Irish peasants to resist their 8,000 landlords in a full-fledged but nonviolent 'land war'. Davitt's father had worked a farm in County Mayo, but after the family was evicted they moved to England, where the boy lost his right arm at a mill job when he was barely 12; he also spent seven years in jail for the Fenian activities. Davitt traveled throughout the United States lecturing and meeting with Irish-American leaders to win support for land reform, and in Ireland his National Land League rallies with Home Rule M.P.s as featured speakers united the causes of social justice and nationalism. When tenants on a Mayo estate decided to join the fight and resist the tyrannical estate manager, Colonel Charles Cunningham Boycott, a new word and a new political tactic were born.

Clan membership in America meanwhile rose from 10,000 in the 1870s to 40,000 by 1880. The Irish National Land League of America was founded to support the Irish movement, and between 1879 and 1882 Americans contributed most of the money — over $5 million — that helped prevent evictions and sustained those Irish families who did lose their farms. American dollars also made it possible for talented young Irishmen,

who had no private incomes of their own because they were not landlords, to serve as Home Rule M.P.s. When Parnell toured the U.S. in 1880 as new head of the Land League, he was welcomed by enthusiastic crowds wherever he went and even addressed Congress. In his speech to the U.S. House of Representatives, he declared, "We must give Irishmen at home a chance to show that energy that has been shown to such an extent in this country. They must own their own land, and govern their own land, free from all foreign influences."

Although Land League officials in Ireland urged farmers to pursue only passive resistance and legal appeals, agrarian protests rapidly developed into violent attacks on landlords, their agents and property. Finally, Prime Minister Gladstone was forced to sponsor the Land Act of 1881, which assured Irish farmers stable tenure at fair rents. With the larger goal of Irish freedom in mind, however, Parnell urged a wait-and-see approach and a no-rent strike; he was sent to Kilmainham Prison, while the government ordered the Land League disbanded. He was finally released after agreeing to support the government's policy in exchange for assistance to

tenants in arrears and an end to coercion.

Now the struggle shifted to the issue of Home Rule. By 1885, Parnell had strengthened his party enough to pursue a new policy of working for the balance of power through an alliance with Gladstone's Liberals. But when Captain William O'Shea sued his wife Katharine for divorce in 1890 and named Parnell as her lover, the Irish leader's political career was ruined. He died of rheumatic fever the following year. The scandal damaged the nationalist cause in Ireland and the United States, lowered morale and split the Home Rule Party so decisively that it was not united until John Redmond, leader of the Parnellite faction, was elected chairman in 1900.

Irish-Americans continued to support and fund the Irish Home Rule Party despite the scandal, although they too were increasingly divided between the segment that backed John Devoy's Clan na Gael and the Land Leaguers led by Bostonians John Boyle O'Reilly and Patrick Collins. During 1884 and 1885 'Dynamite' Dillon and several other extremist Clan members traveled to London and bombed the offices of Scotland Yard and the House of Commons; two of the 'Skirmishers' were killed when they tried to mine London

Bridge. Such acts by men who claimed American citizenship divided the Clan itself and severely strained relations between England and the United States. Yet another ideological split developed in 1891 when the Irish National Federation of America was organized to help win Home Rule for Ireland — a goal Clan leaders Devoy and Judge Daniel Cohalan, who wanted an independent Irish republic, condemned as an 'unworthy compromise'.

Toward the end of the century the American Irish also began to show a renewed interest in their cultural heritage. A new wave of immigrants with strong nationalistic sentiments was arriving, and books like Charles Kickham's *Knocknagow* and T.D. Sullivan's collected *Speeches from the Dock* were popularizing the image of a romantic Ireland filled with courageous, spiritual men and women. Soon a number of organizations were founded whose purpose was to perpetuate Irish-America's language, history and traditions. The New York Society for the Preservation of the Irish Language sponsored concerts of Gaelic songs and promoted study of the language, and following the formation of the Gaelic League in Ireland in 1893, U.S. branches were established to revive both the language and the national culture. Four years later the American Irish Historical Society was organized to document the Irish role in American history.

By the 1890s many Irish-American leaders were expressing this new nationalism by actively urging American politicians to oppose British interests. When the Boer War broke out in 1898, an Irish ambulance corps and an Irish brigade were even recruited in the States to fight for the South African Republic against 'British imperialism'. The following year the four-year-old Irish National Alliance joined with the new National German-American Alliance to oppose U.S. involvement in any unnecessary 'foreign entanglements', particularly a rumored Anglo-American alliance that was supposed to further the cause of colonialism. As victims of British domination, Irish-Americans strongly condemned the U.S. policy of imperialism that emerged from the Spanish-American War, labeling it 'a plant of English growth'. The *Irish World* asked: "Shall Porto Rico become America's Ireland?" By 1908, the Ancient Order of Hibernians had also combined forces with the German Alliance to oppose any British-American rapprochement, and in 1915 Irish- and German-Americans staged protests nationwide, culminating in a massive rally in Madison Square Garden and the formation of a

LEFT *George M. Cohan — the original Yankee Doodle Dandy. Cohan (1878–1942) personified the Irish-American entertainer for more than 50 years through his work as a performer, composer and producer. He is shown here (left) in a scene from the film* Seven Keys to Bald Pate.

joint Irish-German 'Friends of Peace'. Many Germans and Irish demanded that the government end arms sales to the Allies and German propagandists were welcome speakers at many Irish gatherings.

Not all Irish-Americans shared these sentiments, of course, but by 1914 President Wilson had lost patience with those who did. While dedicating a monument to Irish-American John Barry, Wilson praised the naval commander and Revolutionary War hero as an Irishman whose "heart crossed the Atlantic with him", and criticized Americans who "need hyphens in their names because only part of them has come over". The loyalty issue raised by this 'hyphenated Americans' controversy was a major factor in the 1916 presidential race, but Wilson won re-election by a narrow margin.

Once the United States did enter the war against Germany, however, most Americans of Irish descent wholeheartedly supported the war effort, and the famous 'Fighting 69th' again gained fame as one of the first units sent to France. The poet Joyce Kilmer served as regimental historian and was killed on a mission to the front with his celebrated commander, Colonel William 'Wild Bill' Donovan. Rev. Francis Duffy, the regiment's chaplain, was later the subject of a film, and a statue dedicated to him was placed in New York's Duffy Square. Other distinguished Irish-American officers included General John O'Ryan and General Thomas Barry.

Meanwhile, Irish Americans continued to support the struggle for freedom in Ireland. In March 1916, 2,300 delegates gathered at New York's Astor Hotel for a convention of the "Irish Race in America" to "reassert Ireland's claim to nationhood." Barely a month later, events in Ireland gave that claim a searing new urgency. On Easter Monday, April 24, 1916, anticipating German help and largely financed by American Clan monies, nationalist rebels proclaimed a new uprising against British rule. No German aid arrived, however, and the revolt was finally put down by British troops after a week-long siege that destroyed much of central Dublin and killed over 1,500 rebels, soldiers and civilians.

When the leaders of the uprising were executed following wartime military, not civil, trials, Irish-Americans united almost unanimously behind the radical Friends of Irish Freedom. After the end of World War I Clan leaders Devoy and Cohalan organized mass meetings to pressure President Wilson into supporting self-determination for Ireland at the Versailles peace confer-

ence. When he refused to do so on the grounds that he could not interfere in the internal affairs of an ally, the Friends of Irish Freedom launched a campaign to oppose U.S. membership in Wilson's cherished League of Nations, calling it "an instrument to increase the influence of the British Empire in international affairs". The national elections of 1920 were a referendum on both these issues. When Governor James M. Cox of Ohio, the Democratic candidate, lost the race for the Presidency he blamed the 'professional Irish' and his associations with Wilson and the League of Nations.

Although Ireland had been guaranteed Home Rule by a bill passed in 1914, the outbreak of World War I prevented it from being implemented. So when the nationalist Sinn Fein party led by American-born Eamon De Valera, a hero of the 1916 rebellion, won 73 seats in the 1918 parliamentary elections, the victorious candidates refused to go to London. Instead, they formed their own parliament, the Dail Eireann, which proclaimed an Irish republic in January 1919 with De Valera as president. The British arrested the Sinn Fein leaders, but De Valera escaped to the United States and began a new campaign for political and financial support.

Back in Ireland, civil war broke out as 'Black and Tans' fought Sinn Feiners. Irish-Americans, horrified by reports of Black and Tan atrocities and fatal hunger strikes by republican prisoners, staged strikes against British shippers and organized pro-

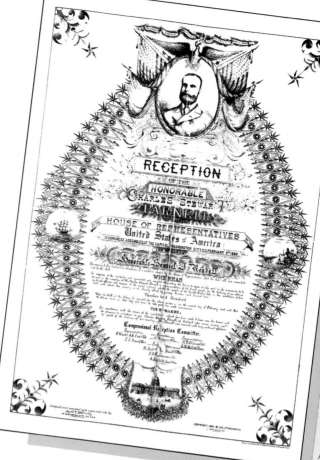

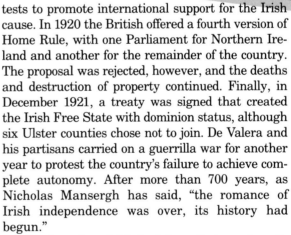

tests to promote international support for the Irish cause. In 1920 the British offered a fourth version of Home Rule, with one Parliament for Northern Ireland and another for the remainder of the country. The proposal was rejected, however, and the deaths and destruction of property continued. Finally, in December 1921, a treaty was signed that created the Irish Free State with dominion status, although six Ulster counties chose not to join. De Valera and his partisans carried on a guerrilla war for another year to protest the country's failure to achieve complete autonomy. After more than 700 years, as Nicholas Mansergh has said, "the romance of Irish independence was over, its history had begun."

The American Irish had done their work well. By 1921, when the Anglo-Irish war of independence ended, they had brought over $5.5 million worth of Irish republican bonds and contributed at least another $5 million in relief funds. But they had gained a lot, as well: an education in the processes of democracy, a clear identity as a people, and finally, pride in having a free homeland "numbered among the nations of the earth", in the words of Robert Emmet. They were also the first group to use the concept of ethnic identity to influence American foreign policy on behalf of a national freedom movement — a tactic that would be adopted by many other minorities who followed him. Now, with their debt to Mother Ireland paid, they could turn their attention to deepening their roots in America.

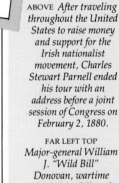

ABOVE *After traveling throughout the United States to raise money and support for the Irish nationalist movement, Charles Stewart Parnell ended his tour with an address before a joint session of Congress on February 2, 1880.*

FAR LEFT TOP *Major-general William J. "Wild Bill" Donovan, wartime chief of the Office of Strategic Services, passes the Swiss Guards after an audience with Pope Pius XII.*

LEFT CENTER *Born in New York to an Irish mother and Spanish father, Eamon De Valera became a professor of mathematics in Ireland and fought in the 1916 Easter Uprising. In 1919, he returned to the United States as President of the newly proclaimed Irish Republic and toured the country to raise funds for the infant nation.*

ABOVE *President-elect John F. Kennedy shaking hands with*
Father Richard J. Casey, pastor of Holy Trinity Catholic
Church in Washington D.C., on the morning of January 20,
1961. Kennedy was inaugurated as the nation's first Catholic
President that afternoon.

Chapter Seven

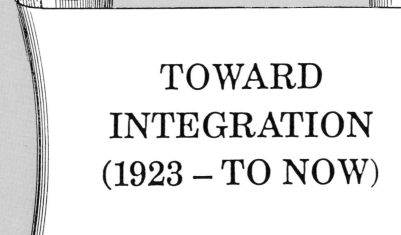

TOWARD INTEGRATION
(1923 – TO NOW)

CHAPTER SEVEN

BELOW RIGHT *Financier and industrialist Andrew William Mellon (1855–1937) was involved in many aspects of American industry, including railroads, steel, insurance and oil. He became Secretary of the Treasury in 1921 and served until 1931 under three Presidents. He was Ambassador to Great Britain in 1931–1932. His personal art collection was donated to the public in 1937 and became the basis for the National Gallery of Art.*

BELOW FAR RIGHT *The first Catholic governor of the state of Massachusetts, David I. Walsh was elected to the Senate in 1918. He was a strong supporter of labor and a vocal opponent of Prohibition.*

uring the 1920s the United States Congress passed the first of several bills that placed numerical limits on immigration — and the great era of the Irish in America began to fade as the era of the American Irish blossomed. The number of Irish immigrants entering the United States dropped from 220,591 in the decade of the 1920s to only 13,167 in the 1930s. The flow picked up after World War II but fell off again in the 1960s, totaling only a little over 120,000. Cities like New York and Boston, which in 1860 had been one-quarter native-born Irish, by 1970 counted fewer than two Irish natives out of every hundred residents. Meanwhile the number of Americans of Irish descent was growing. By the 1950s the grandchildren of Irish immigrants — the third generation — were becoming more representative of the American Irish, and by 1970 members of the third and later generations outnumbered the first and second generations by ten to one. The 1980 census showed only about 200,000 Americans who were actually born in Ireland, but approximately 40.7 million who claimed Irish ancestry, making Irish-Americans the third largest ethnic group in the nation, after those of English and German descent.

As early as the second decade of the new century, however, many Irish-Americans were ready to join the larger society, and Irish neighborhoods disappeared except in the largest cities, like Boston, New York, Chicago and Philadelphia. World War I veterans often moved away after returning from overseas, and Prohibition destroyed the neighborhood saloon, an important community gathering place. The second and third generations were increasingly attending high school; more affluent families were sending their children to Catholic preparatory schools. Occupationally, the Irish were making their mark in a broader range of fields than any other ethnic minority and were well represented in banking and finance, insurance, entertainment, politics and all the professions. Soon exclusive private clubs began to welcome Irish members.

Despite the financial setbacks of the Depression years, the American Irish continued to climb the economic ladder, participating in the post-World War II prosperity that carried many to the suburbs and on to college and graduate school, with help from the G.I. Bill. Today they are more likely than other Americans to be managers or professionals and least likely to be service workers, laborers or factory hands. They produce more than their share of lawyers, medical profes-

CHAPTER SEVEN

LEFT *Many Irish in New York City settled in an area known as Hell's Kitchen. This view of the rear of a typical tenement apartment house on West Fifty-First Street was taken in 1932.*

CHAPTER SEVEN

sionals and scientists, and their success is fast making them as accepted and 'invisible' a part of American society as they choose to be. Even so, the growth of Irish clubs and organizations that began in the late 1960s demonstrates that Irish-Americans are beginning to rediscover and reaffirm their ethnic origins and celebrate the richness and beauty of their cultural heritage.

Although America's Irish quickly mastered the art of urban politics, it took longer for them to achieve prominence in national affairs, particularly with Republican administrations in control during most of the period between the Civil War and the advent of Franklin Roosevelt in 1933. Pierce Butler was appointed a Supreme Court justice in 1923, and Republican Herbert Hoover named William J. 'Wild Bill' Donovan, the World War I hero, Assistant Attorney General and Patrick Hurley Secretary of War. But it was Al Smith's nomination for the Presidency in 1928 that marked the beginning of the Irish ascent to national influence.

Smith was born in 1873 on New York's Lower East Side, in the shadow of the Brooklyn Bridge. His father was a Manhattan teamster who died when Al was only 13, and his mother supported her son and daughter by making umbrellas and running a small grocery store. After quitting school at age 15 he worked for a time in the Fulton Fish Market and then as a laborer at a steam pump plant. In 1903, with the backing of Tammany Hall, he was elected a state assembly-man and served as majority leader, speaker and sheriff of New York County before being elected governor of New York in 1918.

Governor Smith built a reputation as a strong executive, reformer and civil libertarian, but he was the first Catholic ever nominated for the Presidency; his 1928 campaign was marred by smear attacks on his religion and social background as well as his stand against Prohibition. A still predominantly rural America was not yet ready to send a Catholic city boy and machine politician to the White House, and Smith was roundly defeated by Herbert Hoover in a race that left a residue of anger and bitterness among Irish-Americans nationwide. Smith's candidacy created a new national electoral pattern, however, by placing millions of voters, primarily city-dwellers from immigrant families, squarely within the ranks of the Democratic Party. It was their votes that helped elect Franklin Roosevelt in 1932.

Irish-Americans were moving beyond the ethnic neighborhoods mentally as well as physi-

LEFT Four times Governor of New York State, Alfred Emanuel Smith (1873–1944) was born on the Lower East Side of New York City. A popular, crusading reformer, Smith ran on the Democratic ticket in 1928 as the first Roman Catholic candidate for President. He lost to Herbert Hoover.

CHAPTER SEVEN

RIGHT *John Kennedy as he is best remembered: youthful, vigorous, handsome.*

CENTER ABOVE *The ancestral home of the original Kennedys in New Ross, County Wexford, Ireland.*

CENTER BELOW *Senator Robert F. Kennedy of New York announces that he will seek the Democratic nomination for President in 1968. Only a few months later he was the victim of an assassin's bullet.*

LEFT *President John F. Kennedy answers a question at a 1963 press conference.*

LEFT BELOW *The Irish and American flags fly together at Kennedy Memorial Park in New Ross, County Wexford, home of John F. Kennedy's ancestors.*

CHAPTER SEVEN

RIGHT *A youthful Edward Kennedy discusses politics in 1974. Born in 1932, he has been a United States Senator from Massachusetts since 1962. Kennedy is considered the best-informed of all American politicians on Irish questions.*

RIGHT BELOW *Thomas P. "Tip" O'Neill has recently retired after many years as Speaker of the United States House of Representatives. First elected to public office in 1936, O'Neill has never lost an election. On his father's side he traces his ancestry to Mallow, County Cork; on his mother's side, to Buncrana, County Donegal.*

cally. A number of exceptionally talented men of Irish background carried this broader vision with them as they helped to shape the radical social programs of Roosevelt's New Deal. Thomas G. Corcoran of Rhode Island was the most gifted of the President's 'brain trusters' and for several years one of his half-dozen key advisers. James Farley of New York State, who served as Postmaster General, also established the tradition that the chairmanship of the Democratic National Committee should go to an Irish Catholic. As chairman he gave the post new and enduring power and prestige while strengthening the party organization and enlisting its support for the administration's legislative program. Thomas Walsh and later Frank Murphy, a former governor of Michigan, were Roosevelt's choice for Attorney General, and he appointed self-made millionaire businessman Joseph P. Kennedy of Boston Chairman of the Securities and Exchange Commission, then of the Maritime Commission and finally Ambassador to Great Britain. Kennedy, the grandson of an Irish immigrant and son of a ward boss from East Boston, was the first Catholic and the first Irishman to be appointed Ambassador to the Court of St. James's, but he later wrote an even larger chapter of American political history when he helped his son John Fitzgerald Kennedy win the nation's highest office.

A Depression-inspired anti-Republican backlash contributed to the growing American strength of the Democratic Party, which sent increasing numbers of Irish-American senators and congressmen to Washington during the 1930s — some the first Democrats elected from their districts in half a century. Representative John W. McCormack of Massachusetts was a major New Deal strategist who actively supported Roosevelt's domestic legislation and interventionist foreign policy; he later led the fight for passage of the Marshall Plan before becoming Speaker of the House in 1961.

Many of the New Deal programs were first advocated by another Irish-American, Father Charles E. Coughlin, whose national radio broadcasts from the Shrine of the Little Flower in Royal Oak, Michigan, prepared listeners steeped in the doctrine of success through self-reliance to support government intervention on behalf of social justice. A descendant of immigrants from County Cork, Father Coughlin made his first broadcast in 1926 to denounce Ku Klux Klan violence against his church. He was an immediate success and his radio congregation grew steadily, particularly among listeners seeking guidance

CHAPTER SEVEN

LEFT *The first woman to be elevated the United States Supreme Court, Sandra Day O'Connor has had a distinguished judicial career. Her Irish ancestry can be traced to County Tipperary. Her maiden name is a version of O'Dea, a common last name in Ireland.*

LEFT BELOW *Richard M. Nixon, the nation's 37th President, takes the oath of office in 1969. Mrs. Nixon holds two family Bibles as Chief Justice Earl Warren presides. Former President Lyndon B. Johnson is at left.*

CHAPTER SEVEN

BELOW RIGHT During his campaign for the Democratic presidential nomination in 1968, Senator Eugene McCarthy is serenaded by bagpipes as he arrives in Milwaukee on St. Patrick's Day.

and reassurance after the economic collapse of 1929. But his limited knowledge of politics and finance led him to advocate a number of ill-founded conspiracy theories involving 'international bankers' and businessmen and the banking system itself, and after 1938 his attacks on Jews touched off serious street fighting in Dorchester, Massachusetts and the Bronx and Brooklyn in New York. He was finally silenced in 1940 by dwindling financial support and pressure from Archbishop Mooney and other churchmen.

Although the Civil War in Ireland had ended in 1923, the Irish Republican Army had simply taken its battle against partition underground. Irish-Americans, however, were less preoccupied with events in Ireland than with assimilation at home and, after 1929, with economic survival. During the late 1930s, the illegal IRA renewed its attacks with a bombing campaign in Britain. After Ireland declared its neutrality in World War II, 129 leading Irish-Americans cabled Premier De Valera in 1941 to request that he allow Britain the use of Irish air and naval bases in the fight against Nazi Germany. Many others rejected any such proposal, however, and the American Friends of Irish Neutrality was formed to oppose Irish involvement in the war. The same year General O'Ryan and other noted Irish-Americans organized the Committee for American Irish Defense and published an open letter to President Roosevelt which assured him that "You can count on the Irish, Mr. President". They also recommended the establishment of American air and naval bases in Ireland. *The Gaelic American,* however, denounced both the cablegram to De Valera and the committee.

CHAPTER SEVEN

LEFT AND FAR LEFT
*Ballyporeen, County
Tipperary, is proud to
be the ancestral home
of President Ronald
Reagan. On the main
street in Ballyporeen
are the Post Office,
headquartered in
Russell's grocery shop,
and the Ronald Reagan
Lounge, part of John
O'Farrell's pub.*

BELOW LEFT *Senator
Joseph Biden from
Delaware is Irish on
his mother's side. His
political hero is Irish
patriot Wolfe Tone.*

CHAPTER SEVEN

RIGHT *The senior senator from New York, Daniel Patrick Moynihan traces his lineage to County Kerry. A close friend of Irish prime minister Garret FitzGerald, Moynihan is well-versed in his Irish heritage.*

RIGHT CENTER *President Ronald Reagan traces his Irish ancestry to his great-grandfather, Michael O'Regan of Ballyporeen, County Tipperary, who emigrated to America during the famine years. He is shown here being sworn in as the nation's 40th President.*

BELOW RIGHT *Dr. Thomas A. Dooley, born in St. Louis in 1927, served in Southeast Asia as a Catholic medical missionary for many years. He came to national attention in 1954 when he oversaw the treatment of thousands of refugees from North Vietnam. In this photo he is shown with children at a hospital he founded in Laos. Dr. Dooley founded Medical International Corporation, now a part of CARE, to provide medical care in remote areas. He died in 1961.*

CHAPTER SEVEN

LEFT *Hugh Carey was first elected to the House of Representatives for New York in 1961. He served there with distinction until elected Governor of New York in 1975. Carey stepped down after two terms in 1983.*

BELOW LEFT *Terence Cardinal Cook (1921–1983), shown here in 1972 with New York City mayor John Lindsay, was named Archbishop of New York in 1968 and Cardinal in 1969.*

CHAPTER SEVEN

When the United States entered the war after a Japanese attack on Pearl Harbor, the nation's Irish community once again rallied to her defense. Although some Irish-Americans resented the Irish Free State's continued neutrality, President Roosevelt warned Britain that any attempt to coerce the De Valera government would be detrimental to U.S.–British relations. Over 175,000 Irish men and women served in the Allied forces, and Irish-Americans took pride in such celebrated war heroes as Captain Colin Kelly, the war's first Congressional Medal of Honor winner, and General Anthony McAuliffe. The general's succinct response at Bastogne to a German demand that he surrender — 'Nuts!' — demonstrated the famous Irish courage and determination, if not their legendary eloquence.

Irish-Americans continued to hold positions of responsibility in the federal government during the 1940s and 1950s. James Byrnes, whose Irish parents had settled in South Carolina, served in the Senate and on the Supreme Court before becoming Secretary of State. Maurice Tobin was appointed Secretary of Labor by President Truman, and J. Howard McGrath and later James McGranery were named Attorney General. President Eisenhower chose Martin Durkin, the head of the Plumbers' Union, to be his Secretary of Labor, and David I. Walsh, an Irish-American from Boston, was elected to the Senate after serving as Massachusetts' first Catholic governor.

Once the war was over, a number of America's Irish again took up the cause of Irish unity. Under the auspices of the American League for an Undivided Ireland, an Irish Race Convention met in 1947 at the Commodore Hotel in Manhattan. De Valera toured major American cities during the spring of 1948 to speak against partition, and the House Committee on Foreign Affairs agreed to hold hearings on the subject that year and again in 1950. In 1949 the Irish Republic was declared a fully sovereign nation superseding the Irish Free State. Congressman John E. Fogarty of Rhode Island introduced a resolution advocating a political federation of Northern Ireland and the newly proclaimed Irish Republic, unless a majority of all the citizens of the island voted otherwise. Congress considered the resolution in 1951 but rejected it by a vote of 206 to 139. Then the Korean War again diverted attention from the Irish issue, although a renewal of IRA raids and bombings during the mid-1950s foreshadowed the violence that would shatter Northern Ireland 15 years later.

The early 1950s were a period of heightened political tensions in the United States as well,

LEFT *The American Irish have strong attachments to their ancestral land. Here John Lawe, head of the Transport Workers Union of New York City, addresses an Irish Solidarity Day rally in 1983. The rally was held to show Irish-American support for the reunification of Ireland and Irish human rights.*

CHAPTER SEVEN

RIGHT *Cardinal John H. O'Connor was born in Philadelphia in 1920. He takes a strong, sometimes controversial, interest in Irish affairs, and has visited North Ireland to report on justice for the Catholic minority there.*

LEFT *To those of Irish descent, John Ford (1895–1973) is best remembered as the director of the 1952 film* The Quiet Man. *He won an Academy Award for* The Informer *in 1953. Ford directed many Westerns, including the classics* Rio Grande *(1950) and* The Searchers *(1956).*

CHAPTER SEVEN

where Wisconsin Senator Joseph McCarthy provoked a national crisis of confidence that destroyed Secretary of State Dean Acheson, helped defeat the Truman administration and ruined the careers of countless diplomats and other federal employees. Without ever presenting any concrete evidence to support his charges, the farmer's son and Marquette Law School graduate managed to convince many Americans still reeling from World War II and fearful of the developing cold war with Russia that their government, the media and other respected institutions were infested with Communists and Communist sympathizers. His demagogic attacks on intellectuals and other innocent victims finally provoked an official condemnation by the Senate in December 1954, eight years after his election and almost four years after his first anti-Communist speech. But in the interim his crusade had divided the Irish-American community. McCarthy's backing came largely from the old-line working-class neighborhoods in Boston, Brooklyn and Chicago, where many people believed that the fight against Communism was a fight for religious freedom. A majority of the more educated and affluent Irish found his crude, inquisitional tactics offensive. Some Catholic churchmen, including Cardinal Spellman of New York, refused to

condemn him; others, particularly Bishop Bernard Sheil, denounced his narrow, destructive approach to anti-Communism and his "lies, calumny, absence of clarity, and calculated deceit."

John Fitzgerald Kennedy's successful presidential campaign five years later resolved this communal identity crisis by setting a new liberal and intellectual direction in Irish-American politics. A graduate of Choate and Harvard, Kennedy's personal style was marked by candor, courage, energy, wit, and an intelligent, thoughtful approach to the issues. As the grandson of East Boston ward bosses on both sides, he built on the traditional strength of the big-city Democratic machines in his bid to become the nation's first Catholic President. But he also won the trust of many non-Catholics by confronting the issue of separation of church and state head-on: "I do not speak for my church on public matters — and the church does not speak for me".

Kennedy, a decorated naval hero at 29, was elected to the U.S. House of Representatives in 1946; in 1952 he ran for the Senate against Henry Cabot Lodge and won. By 1956 he was ready for a try at the vice-presidential nomination, and despite his defeat by Estes Kefauver he emerged as an exciting new figure on the national political

LEFT *Actor Barry Fitzgerald in* Welcome Stranger, *a 1947 film also starring Bing Crosby and Joan Caulfield.*

CHAPTER SIX

ABOVE *Art Carney and Jackie Gleason as Ed Norton and Ralph Cramden — two ordinary guys from Brooklyn — in the famed television show of the 1950s,* The Honeymooners.

ABOVE RIGHT *Actress Kate Nelligan is Irish-Canadian, but is building an international career. She played a leading role in the film* Eye of the Needle *(shown here) and has also played the female lead in several O'Neill plays, including* Moon for the Misbegotten.

CHAPTER SEVEN

LEFT *Continuing the strong tradition of Irish political clout, William O'Dwyer was Mayor of New York City from 1946 to 1950.*

FAR LEFT *In the 1920s, Bishop Fulton J. Sheen (1895–1979) broadcast* The Catholic Hour *over the radio; starting in the 1950s he had a popular weekly television show called* Life Is Worth Living. *He published more than 50 books. For many years Bishop Sheen was director of the Society for the Propagation of the Faith.*

OPPOSITE BELOW *The personification of the streetwise Irish kid, James Cagney has played many tough-guy roles in such films as* White Heat *and* The Public Enemy. *As shown here, he played George M. Cohan in* Yankee Doodle Dandy. *He also starred in* Shake Hands with the Devil, *playing a professor who joins the IRA. Cagney claims descent from the O'Caignes of County Leitrim.*

scene and a potential presidential candidate. Four years later that promise was fulfilled, and his election marked the triumphant entry of the American Irish into full and equal participation in mainstream American culture.

The Kennedy administration consistently supported liberal democratic principles and used the full weight of its moral authority to advance the cause of civil rights and racial justice. On a visit to his ancestral home in Dunganstown, County Wexford, in 1963 the President reaffirmed his own ethnic roots, but his assassination later that year in Dallas, Texas, cut short any hopes for an officially sponsored solution to the problem of partition. Five years later his brother and political heir, Senator Robert F. Kennedy, was also assassinated after becoming a candidate for President, leaving only Ted, the youngest Kennedy brother and senator from Massachusetts, to carry on the family tradition of political liberalism and committed moral leadership.

Soon after Catholics in Northern Ireland renewed their own struggle for civil rights in 1968, rioting broke out. The violence escalated, and by 1970 the Irish Republican Army had revived its guerrilla war to end the political division of Ireland. With leadership from first-generation residents, Irish-Americans responded to requests for financial and moral support from Irish civil rights leaders by forming chapters of Irish Northern Aid

and other organizations. Fighting spread between British troops and the IRA after hundreds of Ulster Catholics were jailed without trials in August 1971. Irish-Americans staged protests and demonstrations to demand that the U.S. government intervene and force Britain to negotiate a settlement. The events of 'Bloody Sunday', January 30, 1972, brought a new sense of outrage and urgency to opponents of partition when British soldiers fired into a crowd of Catholic demonstrators in Londonderry and killed 13 of them. Spokesmen in the U.S. Congress pressed for concessions from Britain. The London government offered to make amends, but guerrilla warfare continued and Irish-Americans increased their protests and their shipments of money and arms. By 1976 the British government estimated that up to 85 percent of the weapons shipped to the IRA in Northern Ireland were bought in the United States with contributions from the American Irish community, which also gave between $2 million and $3 million to assist the families of IRA men. The deaths of Bobby Sands and 10 other prisoners while on a hunger strike in 1981 deepened animosities in Northern Ireland and further inflamed Irish-American opinion. In Congress, however, the pragmatic 'Friends of Irish Freedom' took a decidedly moderate stand on the Irish question. Led by Senator Daniel Patrick Moynihan of New York, Speaker Thomas P. 'Tip'

CHAPTER SEVEN

RIGHT *Maureen O'Sullivan played opposite Johnny Weissmuller in several Tarzan films. She is the mother of actress Mia Farrow.*

O'Neill and Massachusetts Senator Ted Kennedy, they vehemently opposed violence while remaining committed to righting the wrongs suffered by the Catholic minority in Northern Ireland.

In November 1985, after more than 2,500 had died in the 17 years of renewed civil strife, British Prime Minister Margaret Thatcher and Irish Prime Minister Garret FitzGerald met at Hillsborough Castle, south of Belfast, and signed an accord which gives the Irish government an official voice in the affairs of Northern Ireland. By creating a British–Irish 'Intergovernmental Conference', the agreement affords the south a formal role there for the first time since 1925. Provincial leaders on both sides opposed the accord, but it nonetheless raises hopes for a gradual end to terrorism and improved relations between Protestants and Catholics.

If the majority of American Irish applauded the birth of the Irish Free State and then lost touch with their homeland until the renewal of hostilities in 1968, it was probably because they were so intensely involved in building a life for themselves in America. From the 1920s on, Irish-Americans maintained their leadership in traditional careers such as politics, the Church, labor, sports and business while gaining new prominence in literature, entertainment and the arts. Many made significant and lasting contributions to their fields, and some even became household words.

A number of Irish-American bosses remained powerful figures in urban politics after 1920, including Frank Hague of Jersey City, Thomas J. Pendergast of Kansas City, David L. Lawrence of Pittsburgh and Edward J. Kelly of Chicago. Kelly's successor, Richard J. Daley, was universally regarded as the 'last of the bosses' and occupied the mayor's office in Chicago from 1955 until his death in 1976 — after which his machine organization passed into non-Irish hands.

Irish-American politicians were also at the heart of minority group coalitions that made possible Roosevelt's New Deal, Truman's Fair Deal, Kennedy's New Frontier and Johnson's Great Society. Senator Eugene McCarthy of Minnesota was a staunch supporter of liberal causes and a candidate for the Democratic presidential nomination during the 1960s. Long-time Senator Majority Leader Mike Mansfield now serves as U.S. Ambassador to Japan. County Mayo-born lawyer Paul O'Dwyer participated in all the major civil rights struggles in Ireland and America and served as New York City Council president in the 1970s, and Supreme Court Jus-

tice Hugo Black, of Scotch-Irish ancestry, served for 34 years until his retirement in 1971. Sandra Day O'Connor, the first female Supreme Court justice, is the descendant of Famine immigrants from Tipperary who spelled their name 'O'Dea'.

Today voters have entrusted many of the nation's top offices to Irish-Americans, most notably President Ronald Reagan. The great-grandson of farmhand Michael O'Regan (or O'Riagain), another Famine immigrant from Tipperary, Reagan returned to Ireland for an official visit in 1984. House Speaker Thomas P. 'Tip' O'Neill of Massachusetts, the second most powerful Irish-American politician in the United States, traces his ancestry to County Cork on his father's side and County Donegal on his mother's. Colorado Senator Gary Hart and senior New York Senator Daniel Patrick Moynihan are also both of Irish descent.

Politically the American Irish as a whole remain active campaigners and contributors and have a higher level of overall participation than any other ethnic group. They are more likely to vote, work in community political organizations and keep in touch with their political leaders than other Americans. Even though they have more than solved the problems they faced as immigrants, their enthusiasm for politics remains strong.

CHAPTER SEVEN

LEFT *Gene Kelly in* On The Town. *The legendary dancer/singer/actor can trace his Irish ancestry back several generations on both sides. He won an Academy Award in 1951 for his role in* The Devil Makes Three. *He was named Catholic actor of the year in 1981 by the Catholic Actors Guild.*

RIGHT *Grace Patricia Kelly, also known as Grace, Princess Consort of Monaco. Born in Philadelphia in 1929, she was an established film star (she won an Academy Award in 1954 for* The Country Girl) *when she met Prince Rainier III of Monaco. Their storybook romance led to marriage in 1956. Princess Grace died suddenly in 1982.*

CENTER ABOVE *Greer Garson with Walter Pidgeon in the title role of the 1945 film* Madame Curie.

CENTER BELOW *The great-grandfather of director John Huston came to America from County Armagh in 1840. In 1964, Huston moved permanently back to Ireland and became an Irish citizen. The director of such legendary films as* Moby Dick *and* The Mackintosh Man, *his most recent movie is* Prizzi's Honor.

Prologue

THE IRELAND
THEY LEFT

RIGHT *Actor/director Robert Redford has played many hit roles in films such as* Butch Cassidy and the Sundance Kid *and* The Great Gatsby.

CENTER RIGHT *Best known for his portrayals of both John and Robert Kennedy in television movies, Martin Sheen has also played a number of other Irish roles. His real name is Ramón Estevez; his mother, Mary Ann Phelan, was from County Tipperary.*

LEFT *John Wayne and Maureen O'Hara in the 1952 film* The Quiet Man. *Born Marion Michael Morrison in 1906, John Wayne became one of the world's most popular and recognizable movie stars. He died in 1979.*

BELOW LEFT *One of a rising new generation of young Irish actors, Sean Penn has been seen recently in the films* Racing with the Moon *and* Bad Boys.

RIGHT *Comedian George Carlin grew up in an Irish neighborhood in New York City. He uses his Irish heritage as the basis for many of his comic routines.*

CENTER ABOVE *Actor Jack Nicholson is perhaps best known for his portrayal of Randall Patrick McMurphy, the central character in the movie* One Flew Over the Cuckoo's Nest. *He has won two Academy Awards. Nicholson's paternal grandfather came to America from County Cork.*

CENTER BELOW *Actor Mel Gibson was born in New York, the son of an Irish railway worker, but moved to Australia as a child. Though technically not an Irish-American, the star of* Road Warrior *(shown here) and many other films visits the States often.*

They also continue their active leadership in the Catholic Church. Despite a steady decline in their church membership after 1920, and although today they comprise less than 20 percent of American Catholics, Irish-Americans still provide the Church with more than a third of its clergy and half of its hierarchy. The majority of Catholic Irish-Americans are politically liberal, and a number of Irish churchmen have worked actively for social justice. Monsignor John A. Ryan, the son of a poor Minnesota farm couple originally from County Tipperary, wrote the classic study *A Living Wage.* During the 1920s, as director of the National Catholic Welfare Council's Social Action Department, he developed guidelines far ahead of their time for attacking the problems of unemployment, old-age insurance, and other social issues. Bishop James P. Shannon marched through Selma, Alabama, with hundreds of other priests and nuns in 1965 to win social justice for blacks, and Timothy Cardinal Manning of Los Angeles, a native of County Cork, backed Cesar Chavez in his attempts to unionize Mexican-American agricultural workers in California during the late 1960s. The brothers Daniel and Philip Berrigan, third-generation Irish-Americans on their father's side, publicly protested American involvement in the Vietnam war. Daniel was the first priest to receive a federal sentence; he served 18 months in prison for destroying draft records at a Maryland office of the Selective Service.

Two churchmen of Irish-American descent who

LEFT *Actor Brian Dennehey recently starred in the film* Silverado. *His parents are from County Cork.*

BELOW LEFT *Mia Farrow starred with Robert Redford in* The Great Gatsby.

became well-known media personalities are Bishop Fulton J. Sheen and Dr. Norman Vincent Peale. Bishop Sheen broadcast *The Catholic Hour* on radio during the 1920s; his weekly television series, *Life Is Worth Living,* which aired during the 1950s, was based on his best-selling book of the same name. Dr. Peale, for decades pastor of New York's Marble Collegiate Church, an inspirational author, radio broadcaster and lecturer, is perhaps most famous for his book *The Power of Positive Thinking.* Leading Catholic churchmen today include John Cardinal O'Connor of New York and Bishop Mark Hurley of Santa Rosa, California, a descendant of immigrants from County Cork and the most active clerical spokesman on the Irish question in the United States. Both have visited Ireland as members of a U.S. bishops' delegation.

Even though Irish-Americans were moving up the occupational ladder after 1920, they continued to work as leaders and organizers in the American labor movement. Mike Quill founded the Transport Workers Union of America and served as its first president, and Joe Curran, born to a poor Irish family on New York's East Side, organized sailors along the Atlantic seaboard during the 1930s. In 1937 he became the first

LEFT *One of the most famous faces in television, Ed Sullivan was emcee of his own variety show for many years. An appearance on his show could propel a performer to instant fame — as it did the Beatles. Sullivan, who died in 1975, was active in Irish-American and Catholic affairs.*

FAR LEFT *TV host Mike Douglas — born Michael Delaney Dowd.*

BELOW LEFT *Four-time Emmy Award winner Carroll O'Connor is internationally known for his role as television's Archie Bunker (he is shown here with his co-star Maureen Stapleton). He studied at the National University in Dublin and acted at the Gate Theatre for several years. His maternal grandfather, who came from Brosna, County Cork, was a founder of* The Irish Advocate, *a weekly Irish-American newspaper still published.*

president of the National Maritime Union. An Irish laborer's son, Philip Muirray, served as head of the Congress of Industrial Organizations (CIO) and helped arrange its merger with the American Federation of Labor — another largely Irish creation — in 1955. William George Meany, the grandson of a Famine immigrant and a former officer of the Plumber's Union, became president of the combined AFL-CIO and was the leading spokesman for American labor until his death in 1979.

Foremost among present-day Irish-American labor leaders is Teddy Gleason, who for more than 20 years has headed the International Long-shoreman's Union. The son of poor immigrants from County Tipperary, Gleason began working on the New York docks at 15, joined the ILA at 19 and took over as leader of the union in 1961. John Law, a native of Roscommon, heads the Transport Workers Union; Patrick Campbell is president of the Carpenters Union; and Tom Donahue, whose parents are Irish, serves as executive secretary of the AFL-CIO.

A wide variety of sports have attracted Irish-American athletes since the 1920s and they have excelled in a number of them: Babe Ruth in baseball, Gerry Cooney in boxing, Mary Meagher in Olympic swimming, John McEnroe and Jimmy Connors in tennis, to name just a few.

Their competitive spirit and urge to win have served the American Irish well in business, too. Entrepreneur Paul Galvin is credited with developing the first commercially successful car radio, which he named 'Motorola'. The company he founded is now one of the world's largest manufacturers of electronics. J. Paul Getty, whose ancestors emigrated from County Down in 1824, made a fortune in the oil industry; his son, Gordon, is today the wealthiest man in America. Dublin-born Tony O'Reilly, a former international rugby player, is president and chief executive officer of the Heinz Food Corporation, the fourth largest company in the United States, and also maintains close ties with Prime Minister Garret FitzGerald's Fine Gael Party.

Certainly among the best-known Americans of Irish descent are those who creativity has enriched the cultural life of the nation, especially its arts and literatures. The 1930s particularly was a decade of major achievement for Irish-American authors, playwrights and film stars, although F. Scott Fitzgerald, one of the greatest authors of the century, is more closely identified with the 'Roaring Twenties' and was only 24 in 1920 when *This Side of Paradise* was published. The first Irish

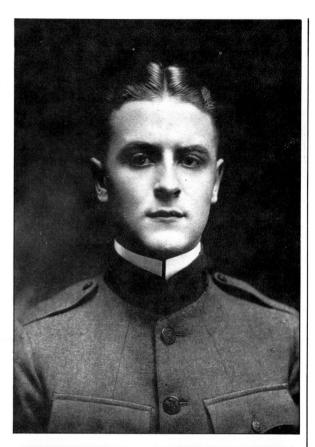

Catholic to become a major American novelist, his book was an instant triumph. The boy from St. Paul, Minnesota, soon became the leading spokesman for the high-living, hard-drinking 'gilded youth' of the Jazz Age. Despite his graduation from Princeton and successful literary career, however, Fitzgerald never lost his fascination with wealth and social standing, and his novels bring an acutely moral vision to bear on the privileged world in which he and his wife Zelda moved. All of his works, but particularly his nearly perfect short novel *The Great Gatsby* and the longer novel *Tender Is The Night,* published nine years later in 1934, brilliantly displayed his talent for social observation, his masterful use of language, his romanticism and also his cynicism.

John O'Hara also won fame with his first novel, *Appointment in Samarra,* published in 1934, and followed it much later with *Butterield 8, Ten North Frederick* and *From the Terrace.* As the son of a small-town doctor from Pottsville, Pennsylvania, his background was also 'lace-curtain' Irish, but his mock Phi Beta Kappa key engraved with the word 'Nope' symbolized that, unlike Fitzgerald, he never attended college or was accepted by the upper-class Protestant establishment he wrote about and longed to join. As a result, the characters he creates to people his fiction are not always emotionally convincing, and his Irishmen are either minor stereotypes or unsympathetic social climbers.

Born and raised the son and grandson of Irish teamsters on Chicago's South Side, novelist James R. Farrell wrote about the neighborhood where he grew up and the poor working men and women who lived there. His brilliant Studs Lonigan trilogy is a classic study of spiritual poverty, while his four novels about Danny O'Neill trace the history of a character who triumphs over the same circumstances.

In 1936 Eugene O'Neill, the son of famed Irish-born actor James O'Neill, became the only American playwright ever to win the Nobel Prize for literature. He spent much of his childhood on tour with his parents, but decided on a career as a playwright only after years of drifting and a serious brush with tuberculosis. Many of his plays portray the family struggles of the Catholic Irish and Protestant Yankees he knew from spending his prep-school years in New England; critics have discerned strong echoes of Irish fatalism and mysticism in his work. O'Neill's acknowledged masterpieces include *Anna Christie, The Emperor Jones, Desire Under the Elms, The Iceman Cometh* and *A Long Day's Journey Into*

LEFT *Novelist and short-story writer Flannery O'Connor (1925–1964) was born in Savannah, Georgia. Her novels include* Wise Blood *and* The Habit of Being. *O'Connor is best known for her grotesque yet often funny portrayals of life in the South.*

LEFT BELOW *The Irish have always been drawn to police and fire service in the cities where they live. Here an enthusiastic New York City corrections officer plays the bagpipes in a parade with his Emerald Society.*

Night. His daughter, Oona, was the wife of famed comedian Charlie Chaplin and the mother of actress Geraldine Chaplin.

During the same period playwright Philip Barry wrote a number of successful romantic comedies, including *The Animal Kingdom* and *The Philadelphia Story.* Actress Laurette Taylor and the Barrymores distinguished themselves on Broadway and in films, while their fellow Irish-American John Ford twice was named best director by the Motion Picture Academy. Other famous entertainers of the era include singing star Bing Crosby, who sold more than 300 million records between 1931 and 1957 and also won an Academy Award for his role as a priest in the 1944 film *Going My Way.* Two years earlier Emmett Kelly, the son of an Irish railroad worker, embarked on a career that was to make him the most famous circus clown in America.

During the 1950s Irish-American entertainers continued to delight audiences both on the screen and in the new medium of television. Jackie Gleason and Art Carney co-starred in the classic comedy series *The Honeymooners;* Gene Kelly carried on the tradition of the Irish song-and-dance man in a score of films; and Greer Garson, Maureen O'Hara, Tyrone Power, James Cagney, Pat O'Brien, Mickey Rooney and John Wayne all have left a lasting imprint on Hollywood cinema. Film star Grace Kelly, later Her Serene Highness Princess Grace of Monaco, was the granddaughter of an immigrant from County Mayo and the daughter of a Philadephia bricklayer's apprentice who rose to become a successful contractor, owner of the largest brickwork company in the United States and a popular figure in Democratic politics. On the other side of the cameras, legendary director John Huston put a new ending on the old saga of Irish emigration by becoming an Irish citizen in 1964, 124 years after his great-grandfather left County Armagh.

Many of today's stars also trace their roots back to Ireland. The mother of actor Martin Sheen was born in County Tipperary, and he has played the Kennedy Brothers, John and Robert, in made-for-television movies. Mel Gibson is the son of an Irish railroad worker who moved his family from New York to Australia when Mel was still a boy, and two-time Academy Award-winner Jack Nicholson's grandfather emigrated from County Cork. Mia Farrow is the daughter of Maureen O'Sullivan, who also had a successful film career, and Sean Penn, Matt Dillon and Aiden Quinn are all young Irish-American movie actors who promise to add to the long list of Irish

successes on stage and screen. Two other popular performers, folksinger Tommy Makem from County Armagh and rock star Van Morrison from Belfast, have also written songs that are classics of their kind.

A number of Irish-Americans have made a name for themselves in broadcasting, including popular talk-show host Phil Donahue, news anchorman Tom Brokaw, and morning-show host Kathleen Sullivan. Four-time Emmy Award–winner Carroll O'Connor, who created the role of Archie Bunker in *All in the Family,* is the grandson of a County Cork immigrant who helped found the still-popular Irish-American weekly *The Irish Advocate.*

Many of the nation's outstanding journalists and authors are also of Irish descent, including syndicated columnists Jimmy Breslin, Pete Hammill and Mary McGrory, poet Galway Kinnell, theologian and educator Mary Daly, and clergyman, social historian and novelist Father Andrew Greeley. Pulitzer Prize–winning novelist William Kennedy was only one of a large number of Irish-Americans whose works have won critical acclaim, among them John Gregory Dunne, Mary McCarthy, Edwin O'Connor, Flannery O'Connor and Wilfred Sheed. *The Subject Was Roses* by Frank Gilroy and *Hogan's Goat* by William Alfred were hits with theatergoers. Working in another medium, painter Georgia O'Keeffe, the granddaughter of a County Cork immigrant, received a Presidential Medal of Honor in 1977. At her death in 1986 at 98 she was acknowledged as a major influence in American art.

America's Irish are now more than 40 million strong, and as their numbers continue to grow, so also do their achievements. But just as they have approached the point of complete integration with mainstream American life, events in Northern Ireland and the newly felt need of many Americans to rediscover their roots have led to a revival of interest in Gaelic culture among Americans of Irish descent. Irish-American institutes and art centers, dance and language classes, gatherings and traditional sports events have sprung up everywhere, and growing numbers of Americans of Irish descent are widening their search for their family origins to include a personal visit to Ireland. As they push our knowledge of the Irish-American experience backward to its beginnings, their ongoing contributions to the life of their adopted homeland are extending it forever forward. It's an exciting story — already more than three hundred years in the telling, and with the end not in sight.

THE LAND THEY
LEFT BEHIND

President Ronald Reagan's ancestors occupied a house on this site in County Tipperary.

PAGES 172/173 *The seacoast of County Wexford, in eastern Ireland, near the ancestral home of the Kennedy family.*

ABOVE *President Ronald Reagan payed a visit to his ancestral home in Ballyporeen, County Tipperary, in 1984.*

ABOVE *Boston Mayor Raymond Flynn, one of the best-known Irish-American politicians in the United States, poses here with a statue of one of his legendary predecessors, Mayor James Curley.*

ABOVE *The Massachusetts State House in Boston, long a symbol of the city and its strong Irish population.*

ABOVE *Cardinal Cooke welcomes His Holiness Pope John Paul II to New York City in 1980.*

ABOVE *Writer F. Scott Fitzgerald combined Irish charm with burning talent to become one of this century's most important novelists. This 1935 portrait hangs in the National Portrait Gallery in Washington, D.C.*

ABOVE *The favourite opponent of Hulk Hogan, the popular
wrestling star, is the Scotsman Rowdy Roddy Piper.*

PAGES 180/181 *The Leam Bridge in Oughterard in County Galway
was the bridge in the film* The Quiet Man, *starring John Wayne.*

ABOVE *Pierce Brosnan, star of the television series "Remington Steele", was born in County Meath. Now a U.S. resident, he still visits Ireland frequently.*

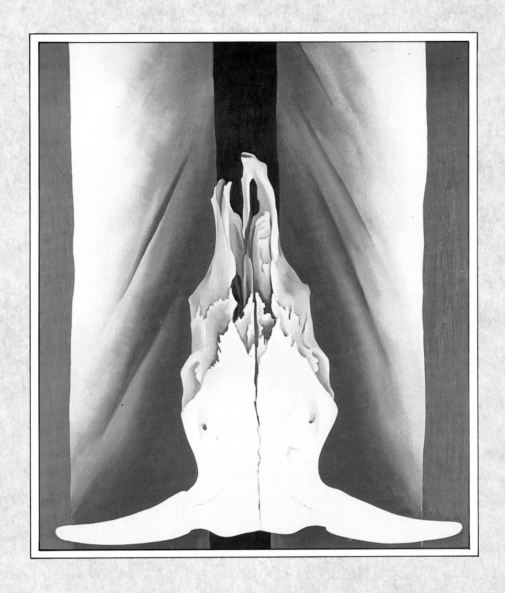

ABOVE *The annual St. Patrick's Day parade in New York City is a chance for the Irish to display their pride in their cultural heritage to the entire nation.*

184

PHOTO CREDITS

BIBLIOGRAPHY

Adams, W.F., *Ireland and Irish Emigration to the New World from 1815 to the Famine* (New Haven: Yale University Press, 1932).

Beckett, J.C., *The Making of Modern Ireland, 1603-1923* (New York: Knopf, 1966).

Birmingham, Stephen, *California Rich* (New York: Simon and Schuster, 1980).

Birmingham, Stephen, *Real Lace: America's Irish Rich* (New York: Harper and Row, 1973).

Breslin, Jimmy, *Forsaking All Others* (New York: Simon and Schuster, 1981).

Breslin, Jimmy, *Table Money* (New York: Simon and Schuster, 1986).

Breslin, Jimmy, *World Without End, Amen* (New York: Simon and Schuster, 1979).

Broehl, Wayne G., *The Molly Maguires* (Cambridge: Harvard University Press, 1964).

Brown, Thomas N., *Irish-American Nationalism* (Philadelphia: J.B. Lippincott, 1966).

Carrol, F.M., *American Opinion and the Irish Question 1910-23* (New York, 1978).

Clark, Dennis, *The Irish in Philadelphia: Ten Generations of Urban Experience* (Philadelphia: Temple University Press, 1974).

Coleman, Terry, *Going to America* (New York: Doubleday, 1973).

Connable, Alfred and Edward Silberfarb, *Tigers of Tammany* (New York: Holt, Rinehart and Winston, 1967).

Curley, James Michael, *I'd Do It Again: A Record of All My Uproarious Years* (Englewood Cliffs, NJ: Prentice-Hall, 1957).

D'Arcy, William, *The Fenian Movement in the United States, 1858-1886* (New York: Russell & Russell, 1971).

Dibble, Roy F., *John L. Sullivan: An Intimate Narrative* (Boston: Little, Brown, 1925).

Diner, Hasia R., *Erin's Daughters in America* (Baltimore: The Johns Hopkins University Press, 1983).

Dunne, Finley Peter, *Mr. Dooley in the Hearts of His Countrymen* (Boston, 1899).

Dunne, Finley Peter, *Observations by Mr. Dooley* (New York, 1902).

Dunne, John Gregory, *Dutch Shea Jr.* (New York: Pocket Books, 1983).

Dunne, John Gregory, *True Confessions* (New York: Pocket Books, 1981).

Ellis, Elmer, *Mr. Dooley's America* (New York: Knopf, 1941).

Ellis, J.T., *Life of James Cardinal Gibbons: Archbishop of Baltimore, 1834-1921* (Milwaukee, 1952).

Farrell, James T., *Studs Lonigan* (New York:1932).

Fitzgerald, F. Scott, *The Great Gatsby* (New York: Scribner's, 1920).

Fitzgerald, F. Scott, *This Side of Paradise* (New York: Scribner's, 1920).

Flanagan, Thomas, *The Year of the French* (New York: Holt, Rinehart and Winston, 1979).

Greeley, Andrew M., *That Most Distressful Nation* (Chicago: Quadrangle Books, 1973).

Greeley, Andrew M., *The Irish-Americans: The Rise to Money and Power* (New York: Harper and Row, 1981).

Greeley, Andrew M., *Thy Brother's Wife* (New York: Warner Books, 1983).

Griffin, William D., *A Portrait of the Irish in America* (New York: Scribner's, 1983).

Handlin, Oscar, *Boston's Immigrants, 1790-1880* (Cambridge: Harvard University Press, 1959).

Joyce, W.L., *Editors and Ethnicity: History of the Irish-American Press, 1848-83* (New York, 1976).

Kahn, E.J., *The Merry Partners: The Age and Stage of Harrigan and Hart* (New York, 1955).

Kennedy, William, *Ironweed* (New York: Viking Press, 1983).

Kennedy, William, *O Albany!* (New York: Viking Press, 1983).

Kinnell, Galway, *Selected Poems* (Boston: Houghton Mifflin, 1983).

Levine, E.M., *The Irish and Irish Politicians* (South Bend: University of Notre Dame Press, 1966).

Lyons, F.S.L., *Ireland Since the Famine* (New York: Scribner's, 1971).

Maguire, John F., *The Irish in America* (New York: Arno, 1974; original edition, 1868).

McAvoy, T.T., *History of the Catholic Church in the United States* (South Bend: University of Notre Dame Press, 1969).

McCaffrey, Lawrence J., *The Irish Diaspora in America* (Washington, D.C.: The Catholic University of America Press, 1984).

McCaffrey, Lawrence J., *The Irish Question, 1800-1922* (Lexington, KY: University of Kentucky Press, 1968).

McCarthy, Mary. *Memories of a Catholic Girlhood* (New York: Harcourt, Brace Jovanovich, 1957).

McGee, Thomas D'Arcy, *History of the Irish Settlers in North America* (New York: Oxford University Press, 1985).

Miller, Kerby A., *Emigrants and Exiles: Ireland and the Irish Exodus to North America* (New York, Oxford University Press, 1985).

Niehaus, Earl F., *The Irish in New Orleans, 1800-1860* (Baton Rouge: Louisiana State University Press, 1965).

O'Brien, Michael J., *A Hidden Phase of American History: Ireland's Part in America's Struggle for Liberty* (New York: Dodd, Mead and Co., 1920).

O'Connell, William Cardinal, *Recollections of Seventy Years* (Boston: Houghton, Mifflin, 1934).

O'Connor, Edwin, *The Last Hurrah* (Boston: Little, Brown, 1956).

O'Connor, Flannery, *The Complete Stories* (New York: Farrar, Straus and Giroux, 1971).

O'Faolain, Sean, *King of the Beggars: A Life of Daniel O'Connell* (New York: Viking Press, 1938).

O'Grady, Joseph P., *How the Irish Became American* (New York, Twayne, 1973).

O'Grady, Joseph P., *Irish-Americans and Anglo-American Relations, 1880-88* (New York, 1976).

O'Hara, John, *Pal Joey* (New York: Random House, 1983).

O'Neill, Eugene, *The Later Plays* (New York: Random House, 1967).

O'Neill, Eugene, *Long Day's Journey into Night* (New Haven: Yale University Press, 1950).

O'Neill, Eugene, *Selected Plays* (New York: Random House, 1969).

Potter, George W., *To the Golden Door* (Boston: Little, Brown, 1960).

Schlesinger, Arthur M., *A Thousand Days: John F. Kennedy in the White House* (New York: Fawcett, 1971).

Schrier, Arnold, *Ireland and the American Emigration, 1850-1900* (Minneapolis: University of Minnesota Press, 1958).

Shannon, William V., *The American Irish* (New York: Macmillan, 1963).

Sheed, Wilfred, *The Hack* (New York: Random House, 1980).

Sheed, Wilfred, *People Will Always Be Kind* (New York: Farrar, Straus and Giroux, 1973).

Tansill, Charles Callan, *America and the Fight for Irish Freedom: 1866-1922* (New York: Devin-Adair, 1957).

Wakin, Edward, *Enter the Irish American* (New York: T.Y.Crowell, 1976).

Walsh, J.P., *The Irish: America's Political Class* (New York, 1976).

Walsh, J.P., *The San Fransisco Irish, 1850-1976* (San Fransisco, 1978).

Ward, Alan, *Ireland and Anglo-American Relations, 1899-1921* (London: Weidenfeld and Nicolson, 1969).

Webb, Walter Prescott, *The Texas Rangers* (Boston: Houghton, Mifflin, 1935).

Werner, M.R., *Tammany Hall* (New York: Doubleday, Doran & Co., 1928).

White, Theodore H., *The Making of the President, 1960* (New York: Atheneum, 1961).

Wittke, Carl, *The Irish in America* (Baton Rouge, Louisiana State University Press, 1956).

INDEX